I0158304

THEOLOGY OF THE CROSS

THEOLOGY OF THE CROSS

LUTHER'S *HEIDELBERG DISPUTATION* AND
REFLECTIONS ON ITS 28 THESES

———

TRANSLATION BY CALEB KEITH

EDITED BY CALEB KEITH AND KELSI KLEMBARA

1517 Publishing

Theology of the Cross: Luther's Heidelberg Disputation and Reflections on Its 28 Theses
© 2018 Kelsi Klembara and Caleb Keith

All rights reserved. No part of this publication may be reproduced, distributed, or transmitted in any form or by any means, including photocopying, recording, or other electronic or mechanical methods, without the prior written permission of the publisher, except in the case of brief quotations embodied in critical reviews and certain other noncommercial uses permitted by copyright law. For permission requests, write to the publisher at the address below.

Published by:
1517 Publishing
PO Box 54032
Irvine, CA 92619-4032

Publisher's Cataloging-In-Publication Data
(Prepared by The Donohue Group, Inc.)

Names: Klembara, Kelsi, editor. | Keith, Caleb, editor. | Luther, Martin, 1483–1546. Disputatio Heidelbergae habita. English.
Title: Theology of the Cross : Luther's Heidelberg disputation and reflections on its 28 theses / edited by Kelsi Klembara & Caleb Keith ; translated by Caleb Keith.
Description: Irvine, CA : 1517 Publishing, [2018] | Includes an original translation of Luther's Heidelberg disputation.
Identifiers: ISBN 9781948969055 (softcover) | ISBN 9781948969062 (ebook)
Subjects: LCSH: Luther, Martin, 1483–1546. Disputatio Heidelbergae habita. | Luther, Martin, 1483–1546—Criticism and interpretation. | Religious disputations—Germany. | Theology of the cross. | Jesus Christ—Crucifixion.
Classification: LCC BR332.5 .T44 2018 (print) | LCC BR332.5 (ebook) | DDC 230/.41/092—dc23

Printed in the United States of America

Cover design by Brenton Clarke Little.

CONTENTS

A BRIEF TRANSLATOR'S PREFACE

CALEB KEITH

The theology of the cross is one of the core elements of Martin Luther's theology. The development of this doctrine through the *Heidelberg Disputation* has been considered an essential element of Luther's breakthrough on justification,[1] and crucial to his theological reforms and future split with the Roman Catholic church. Inspired by the 500th anniversary of Luther's presentation at Heidelberg, I began studying the subject of Luther's *theologia crucis* or theology of the cross. As I began to read the 28 theses and their proofs, I found the handful of translations available lacking. While technically accurate, the style and flow of these translations is abrupt and, at times, confusing. I was often left to re-read sections several times to get at the basic meaning. This is rather unfortunate since much of the profundity of the *Heidelberg Disputation* is due to its brevity and clarity. Within this early work, Luther tackles the benefit and function of God's Law, the bondage of the will, the problem of evil, the grace and

---

[1]Alister McGrath, *Luther's Theology of the Cross: Martin Luther's Theological Breakthrough,* 2nd ed. (Oxford: Blackwell Publishing Ltd., 2011).

love of God, the Christological implications of the cross, and even Christian living.

For my translation, I attempted to get at the heart of these ideas as expressed in the Latin text but with maximum readability. Luther's theses are pointed and witty; I hope that such an ethos comes through in this edition. Furthermore, to achieve a translation style leaning toward accessibility, I also had to make a handful of theological decisions. The prime example deals with the word *iustus*. This word can mean both justified and righteous. While older translations tend to only use *righteous,* there are key instances where I believe justified to be more contextually appropriate. Particularly in instances where Luther is obviously referring to Christian believers, I understand justified to be a better translation in order to emphasize Luther's point that there are no righteous people apart from the justification brought about by the suffering of the cross.

There is some debate as to whether Luther had begun to think of justification in terms of imputation at this early of a point in the Reformation. However, I follow along with McGrath's argument that in fact, Luther had begun making moves to this distinction beginning as early as 1514 and developed through his many *disputatio* and lectures leading up to 1518–1519. Considering the content of the *Heidelberg Disputation* and the consensus of Forde, and Barone[2] on this issue, I find that the research is in favor of this shift toward

---

[2]Marco Barone, *Luther's Augustinian Theology of the Cross: The Augustinianism of Martin Luther's Heidelberg Disputation and the Origins of Modern Philosophy of Religion* (2017), 1.

justification. There are also other terms which are either expanded or modernized in the translation, often the literal translation or older term will be present in the footnotes for clarity.

Finally, as part of my translation work, certain patterns arise very quickly. Forde somewhat famously recognized four main categories within the text: Theses 1–12 as the conflict between God's righteousness and human works, Theses 13–18 as the failure of human will to avoid sin, Theses 19–24 as the divide between glory and the cross, and Theses 25–28 as the re-creation of sinners into believers.[3] Forde's distinctions capture the essence of Heidelberg and how the cross is the center of all doctrine from beginning to end. For the purposes of this work, I thought it would be beneficial to break things down into even smaller pairs than Forde does in order to highlight the immediate contrasts which Luther crafted within neighboring theses. In many instances, the full weight of a thesis does not strike separately but is more complete when read with others in groups of two or three. Again, it is my goal that this methodology brings the words of hope so purposely proclaimed by the cross to as many people as possible.

---

[3]Gerhard O. Forde, *On Being a Theologian of the Cross: Reflections on Luther's Heidelberg Disputation, 1518* (Grand Rapids: Eerdmans, 1997).

AN INTRODUCTION TO THE
HEIDELBERG DISPUTATION

STEVEN PAULSON

Luther's *Heidelberg Disputation* astounded its hearers in 1518 and has not ceased shaking the world's foundations since. By rights, this should have been one more in a series of dull theological lectures among other routine business at the Augustinian Order's General Chapter meeting. The one notable thing going in was that Luther was expected to take the opportunity in his lecture to recant some of his wilder of the *95 Theses* and come to heel like an obedient friar. But Luther was now not only a friar but a teacher of the whole church, and instead of splitting hairs and walking back, as theologians are accustomed to do, Luther opened both barrels and delivered an astounding set of "provocations" that were meant to "root out completely the Canon Law, scholastic theology, philosophy and logic as they are now taught." No small task! Why merely drain the swamp when you can flood the thing? So when his time came, Luther didn't even bother mentioning "indulgences" but instead laid into Aristotle, Thomas, Ockham and the whole kit and caboodle of university teachers, canon lawyers, and church leaders. Yet he did it so calmly and kindly, and showed such great patience with his stupefied brothers, that people could hardly grasp what had happened to them.

Many who were present that day were hearing Luther for the first time, and when he unleashed his "paradoxes" their jaws dropped to the ground at the opening line: *the Law of God, which is the most beneficial doctrine of life, is not able to advance man toward righteousness but rather stands against him.* Goodbye monasticism! Goodbye Christian life! Goodbye world order! Afterward, Luther said he left his poor brother hermits, "pensive and dazed." He wasn't sure anyone quite understood the blow he had just dealt. Still, many, like Martin Bucer and Johannes Brenz, would never again let go of Luther because of these paradoxes. The elated Bucer, who never did quite "get it" even as a later magisterial "reformer," wrote back to a friend declaring that he had just found, "one who has got so far away from the bonds of the sophists and the trifling of Aristotle, one who is so devoted to the Bible, and is so suspicious of antiquated theologians of our school . . . that he appears to be diametrically opposed to our teachers . . . (H)e is Martin Luther, that abuser of indulgences . . ." Bucer went on to say that this indulgence abuser "propounded some paradoxes, which not only went farther than most could follow him, but appeared to some heretical." Indeed, Luther recounted that while most participants were bantering back and forth in curiosity about the theses (as theologians do), one young doctor finally blurted out: "If the peasants heard this they would stone you to death!" This broke the tension, and everyone had a good gallows laugh at Luther's expense. Dead man walking! But Bucer went away having memorized three of the theses—the first regarding the end of the Law, the second saying that it was "probable" that all good works are sins, and the third—that free will was "a mere name"! No free will? Who says that?

Luther figured the old hermit codgers in Heidelberg would never absorb this, and like any man before his time, thought his provocations would have to be left to a younger generation to unpack. But that was not at all what happened. In order to do his provoking, Luther created a genre of theology straight out of Scripture that has been associated with Lutherans ever since (for good or ill): the paradox. "The Law says, 'do this,' and it is never done. Grace says, 'believe in this,' and everything is already done" (Thesis 26). No teaching is clearer and no education proceeds more quickly to the heart of its students than the stark black and white (binary) contrast of polar opposites: "A theology of glory calls evil good and good evil. A theology of the cross calls the thing what it actually is" (Thesis 21). As a result, Luther gave us our Lutheran *bona fides*. It is the *cross*, not *glory* that is our theology. It was not Kierkegaard or even Hamann who discovered this contrary communication, this panoply of opposites, by which paradox reveals our foolishness, hypocrisy and sheer opposition to God. It was Luther who created theological paradox in this *Heidelberg Disputation*. Of course, Luther learned it from the masters of paradox themselves, the sarcastic prophets of God: "Hear O Deaf, look you blind" (Is. 42:18), and the unsurpassed irony, mockery, cynicism, acerbity, disdain and scorn of Jeremiah: "They have healed the wound of my people lightly, saying, 'Peace, peace,' when there is no peace" (Jer. 6:14). No wonder Lutherans luxuriate in negation, conflict, and especially self-hatred just as Augustine taught it. What a sense of humor they have, knowing that to God, our futility is funny.

So it is that the major paradox is cross—not glory. The cross is disorienting because it will not give us what we want. It will not measure righteousness by the Law, and then reward it accordingly. Churches, states, and individuals all set up systems of merit, and then apply their legal judgment—and look! We inevitably find ourselves to be good according to our own system and aim to prove that God agrees. Most especially, faith is understood to be a work in process—it is never complete until one reaches the vision of God in glory. Faith is then tempered with doubt lest the spiritual in us loses motivation to keep plodding along. Attacking this glory meant Luther was dismantling the heart of monasticism's system of managed doubt. Some found it so awe-inspiring that it changed their entire lives and careers, indeed, some would go on to die for it. So what is worth dying for in these little provocations?

The collection of interpretations that follow in this book will help you to understand the impact of the theses. But let's take a first glimpse at the counter-intuitive, contrary, offensive, and thrilling paradoxes, starting with the first and most astounding of them all: "The Law of God, the most salutary doctrine of life, cannot advance humans on their way to righteousness, but rather hinders them." God's Law is the best thing we have for preserving life—but this divine Law not only fails to elevate peoples' righteousness but actually hinders their rise. Of course, Paul was familiar with the paradox: the Law does not remedy sin, it makes sin greater (Rom. 5:20). Why then would God give the Law? Luther labels the offense of this question our inbred yearning for the "theology of glory."

Glory theology assumes a set of things that we sinners think are "common sense." First, that I, as a human being, once had glory like God's (*imago dei*). When God gave a command my immortal soul would respond with joy and dutiful obedience as to a beloved Father or King. However, secondly, while God liked obedience, He supposedly did not want robots or puppets so He gave souls their highest power—a free will. Third, unfortunately, my soul followed the sad procession of souls that freely chose disobedience and so fell out of heaven into the physical world with its bodily desires. Finally, my whole life since has been an arduous journey back to the glory I lost. But, because my body is laden with lowly desires, this return to my soul's original state cannot happen without much help in the form of grace. I can access this grace from Christ both from following his example of perfect obedience, and by partaking of his sacramental infusion of merit that empowers me to climb the ladder back to my former glory. In that great day, I will once again have the choice of doing or not doing the Law but will get it right this time.

Glory is simple and infectious. It has everything I need: the Law, my free will, and the struggle to climb back into heaven. But in the middle of my dream, starting 500 years ago, the little Friar Luther took my dream away. Not only did he remove it, but then proceeded to heap dung upon my dream by saying that if the Law cannot help you, good works are even more useless. Giving alms to the poor and making use of the sacrament of repentance—everything you call "good"—is really a mortal sin, and the very thing we call evil is God's real, true work—an eternal merit. In fact, up to this point in the paradoxes, Luther was preaching to the choir, since hermits and fanatics all love negation, guilt, self-hatred, and humility. But here is where Luther gets really interesting. What is the thing in this life that we have, up to now, called evil, but which is, paradoxically, God's own holy work—an eternal merit? What is it that we hate more than anything in life? Is it people being selfish? Is it people being greedy? Is it people who do not really try to resist bodily desires like we Christians do? No. We think evil is God up and forgiving a sinner without anything asked of them before or after. In all their efforts at pleasing God, glory seekers think that God's Gospel is the one truly evil thing in life! What about striving? Forgiveness cuts out our whole spiritual purpose in life and calls it evil.

So Luther proceeds to the crux of the matter (Theses 19 and 20): that person who claims to see the invisible things of God—through the earthly stuff—constantly confuses evil for good and good for evil. To the contrary, that person who comprehends what is visible of God's backside through suffering and the cross—that one does not make up a fake world, "says what a thing is." Luther then asked, what is this "*what a thing is*" that a theologian of the cross can finally utter? Here Luther was in his own throes of a great trial. The theologian of the cross is not merely humble. The theologian of the cross is not merely a negator, or reverser who looks for the lowly, outcast, downward, oppressed, and dirty in order to discover the true and proper location for God in this world—that is below rather than above. This misunderstanding is simply monasticism 2.0. Calling evil good and good evil is not remedied by merely turning the value system of the world on its head in order to establish a new, negative, contrary, paradoxical value system. If that were what "cross" meant, then if a person is proud of good looks, the true Christian is supposed to become plain, like the Quakers. Or if a person is shunned for her ill behavior in marriage, we should now embrace that negative behavior as God's way of accepting the stranger, the alien, the different, the Other. Such shenanigans are nothing more than the play of a comedian or court jester whose calling is to upset Law and order in order to show the futility of the Law—an inverse, antithetical, dark tradition of self-judgment that at least goes back to Greek dramas. Would-be Lutherans commonly make this mistake that by considering their contrary value system, or solidarity with the poor, the weak, the sinner, the queer, the misunderstood, and the outcast as somehow "cross" as opposed to "glory." They then make cross merely negative glory—and religion is merely a race to see who can love more offensive things than any others.

Even in Luther's day this way of dealing with paradox spawned many such negative theologians of glory, who could not relish enough the flouting of norms, tradition, speaking "truth to power," and taking the side of the underdog and oppressed—not least of them the fanatic Müntzer. This is why Luther says, "Wisdom is not itself evil, nor should the Law be avoided [but without the theology of the cross, man misuses the greatest things as if they were the worst things]" (Thesis 24). How, then do we receive the cross or does the cross become laid upon us? Do we learn to love it, against our own instincts, wants and desires? No. Escaping this black hole of humility required Luther to take his last step that truly understands that the cross is an attack by

God—it is never liked or grasped. You can't love the cross. For this reason, the genre of paradox itself (not works, but faith) is not the heart of the Lutheran teaching, nor is it Luther's own final word on this matter of what we mean by being made into a theologian of the cross. Soon after this disputation, Luther filled in the one missing thing from his apocalyptic rupture of the ages at Heidelberg: "Law says, 'do this,' and it is never done. Grace says, 'believe *in this*'. . . . and all things are already done" (Thesis 26).

What is this "this"? A simple demonstrative pronoun, "this," is meant to say that something is very near to the speaker: Believe this! Bucer and his ilk later got confused about this when Jesus said it at the Last Supper: This is my body! What is "this"? What is so near? Luther's penultimate Heidelberg Thesis tries to fill in the pronoun with the general "the work of Christ." But what exactly is that work? What exactly did the cross achieve? Is it what the church called His merit? The final thesis tries further to provide the missing noun, so "this" means "the love of God." God's love, in delightful paradox, does not desire what is already there in things visible (as we helpless creatures do), but God's love creates what is not. This allowed Luther to dispatch Aristotle's "sleeping god," who taught us that God sets out a Law and waits to see who can complete the journey to fulfill it, and is why throughout the Heidelberg Theses, Luther makes fun of Aristotle/Aquinas. No wonder Luther's own signature at the time was, "Brother Martin Eleutherius, Augustinian." Martin, the free. God is not sleeping, but acting.

But here Luther's discovery of faith—not works—still needed something to believe in. What was God doing that was so evil in our eyes and an assault upon our dreams? How does the cross become our salvation if it is, and always will be, impossible to embrace and love? The dream of American church life, for example, is to embrace "the old rugged cross," but Luther says this is a fraud. The logicians at universities attempt to say you could love the cross by showing how perfectly it fit the system of merit. But they too failed. Likewise, the monks, the pure negators of self and God, facilitated Luther's own final attempt to storm heaven through the mystics Tauler and the unknown Frankfurter. But this too failed.

So it was that as much as the *95 Theses* awakened the world and started the Reformation in October of 1517, the following year was even more consequential to the whole Reformation. Luther was working intensely in the first winter months of 1518 on his *Resolutions* defending his *95 Theses*. Two points emerged that made Luther much more dangerous to them than John Hus ever was. First, the fifty-eighth thesis became the object of ire for saying that *Christ's* merits (the cross) were not the same thing as the merits of *indulgences*. Whatever the "merits of Christ" were, they were not the same thing as a chest of indulgences that the Pope could open and disseminate as the spirit moved him.

Christ's treasure pointed instead to Matthew 16:19 and the office of the keys. Luther was thus getting closer to filling Heidelberg's demonstrative pronouns: "believe this—and it is already done." It has to do with the sacrament of the keys. By the end of 1518, Luther had his second "occasion" for recanting before Cardinal Cajetan at Augsburg. Cajetan could not get past the authority of the pope in this matter, and so it was Peter who received these keys. However, the world's greatest Thomistic expert also saw the writing on the wall with Luther despite whatever role Peter played. The second crucial matter then emerged in the rather innocent looking seventh thesis of the 95 that, "God remits guilt to no one unless at the same time He humbles him in all things and makes him submissive to his vicar, the priest." With this, Luther tapped the spring that would become the fountain of the reformation.

How does God forgive sin in the office of the keys if it is not by means of a mercantile payment doled out by the pope—a buying of Christ with the church as banker? There Cajetan lit on the words that most troubled him about Luther. Everyone who knew Aquinas, or for that matter Lombard (or even Augustine), knew that the remission of sin by a priest was, by church consensus, not to be anything certain or sure. Otherwise, repentance would never be achieved. If Luther were right, a priest who forgives is not giving a penalty whose completion awaits an uncertain future completion. The keys would instead give a direct, unconditional promise that has no reference to the Law or the sinner's intention at all—despite whatever "obex," or obstacle a free will may or may not present. That makes Scripture's justifying faith into God's faithfulness, not our own, and thus faith would be indubitable, with nowhere else to go and nothing else to do. Was Luther saying that with the sacrament comes full assurance—a faith that does not need any other seal, approval, deed, work or fulfillment of Law? Yes, Luther answered, and so he found his missing reference for the pronoun: "believe this."

By the end of the year, Luther was opposing Cajetan's most basic rule of church life—that faith cannot be certain as it comes to the sacrament (or it will never strive). In contrast, Luther was saying a local priest simply gives a release that is bigger than anything the Pope can produce: what is loosed on earth is loosed in heaven so that the very sinner is thereby made completely sure both of God's grace and gift. He thus secures the entire future—the eschaton—in that one little word. Nothing can separate us from the love of God in Jesus Christ. Cajetan concluded that if Luther were correct, and faith meant both coming to and leaving the sacrament doubtless, then the church would no longer be responsible for extracting a payment from those in debt. The mass would not be a sacrifice. The papacy had no other treasure of merit than this. What was the church to be then? Where would its power to judge go? All Luther had in his little church was the absolution and the absolved—nothing more. The keys operate without Law or judge—either the state's or the church's. So faith is right there certain, firmed, and assured with nothing more to add. Believe this, and it is already done.

Luther cleared the deck with his *Heidelberg Disputation*'s paradoxes: not glory but cross. Faith, not work. But by the end of the year, in his trial at Augsburg, Luther finally had an answer for what previously was merely the negation of the monastic humility: the "believe this . . . and it is already done." There is no spiritual journey to glory. There is no grisly learning to love the cross by loving what you formerly hated. The "this" that is Christ's treasure is wherever and whenever a priest takes out the keys of his office and uses them right then and there—and look! It is already done. Righteousness is thereby given by faith alone, without any addition—ever. The cross ends not in our humility, but our assurance because the cross ceases being an object of love and becomes preached to sinners as an inescapable attack on their glory: "On account of Christ's cross, I forgive you." Thus in one golden year, 1518, Luther twice refused to refute his *95 Theses*. In the first, he cleared the deck with the great negation of the paradoxes in the *Heidelberg Disputation*—not Law, not glory, not even love of cross. Then suddenly, the missing noun was supplied for the Gospel: "believe this" was the simple, unshakeable divine promise—the office of the keys with its final word "I forgive you." Luther was then really free without any free will, and faith was finally in something that was sure. Neither the church nor the world has ever been the same in the five hundred years since, thank God, so enjoy the paradoxes, and even more enjoy the Gospel when it comes near.

LUTHER'S *HEIDELBERG DISPUTATION*

28 THESES AND PROOFS

CALEB KEITH

---

1 ══════════════════════════════

THE LAW OF GOD, WHICH IS THE MOST BENE-FICIAL DOCTRINE OF LIFE, IS NOT ABLE TO ADVANCE MAN TOWARD RIGHTEOUSNESS BUT RATHER STANDS AGAINST HIM.

The substance of this statement is made apparent by the Apostle Paul[1] in his letter to the Romans. In Chapter 3, "The righteousness of God has been revealed apart from the law." Augustine explains this in his book, *On the Spirit and the Letter*, "Apart from the Law means apart from its support." Then in Romans 5, "The Law came so that sin might

---

[1] Throughout the text, Luther frequently cites the Pauline epistles and the authority of the Apostle Paul. However, Luther simply refers to Paul as "The Apostle." For clarity, this translation adds the actual name of Paul.

increase." And in Chapter 7, "When the command came, sin came back to life." This is why in Chapter 8, Paul calls the Law, "a law of death" and "a law of sin." This goes even further in 2 Corinthians 3, "The letter lays slaughter," which Augustine understands throughout the entirety of *On the Spirit and the Letter* to apply even to the holiest Law of God.

2

MUCH LESS COULD THE WORK OF MEN, THAT IS TO SAY EVEN WORKS WHICH ARE DONE OVER AND OVER AGAIN WITH THE HELP OF NATURAL LAW, MOVE SOMEONE TOWARD RIGHTEOUSNESS.

God has given the Law to man as holy, spotless, true, just, etc. for the purpose of assisting man beyond his own natural abilities in order to illuminate and move him toward goodness. However, the exact opposite happens in that man steps up to become even more wicked. In what way is man able to advance toward goodness when left to his own might apart from such outside help? If he is not able to move toward goodness with such outside help, he will do even less when left to his own means. Thus the Apostle Paul in Romans 3 declares all men are corrupt and weak, neither do they know God nor do they ask for Him, instead all turn away from Him.

3

EVEN THOUGH THE WORKS OF MAN ALWAYS SEEM TO BE BEAUTIFUL AND GOOD, THEY ARE NEVERTHELESS DEMONSTRABLY DEADLY[2] SINS.

Human works seem beautiful externally, but on the inside they are obscene, thus Christ says to the Pharisees in Matthew 23. For though they and others seem good and beautiful, in fact, God is good and beautiful, who does not judge according to outward appearance, but searches hearts and minds.[3] And so without grace and faith it is impossible to have a clean heart. He cleansed their hearts by faith.[4]

Therefore, the thesis is demonstrated: If the works of justified men are sins then it is asserted that they are much greater sins for those who are not yet justified. But the just speak on behalf of their works: do not begin to judge your

---

[2]Luther's *Heidelberg Disputation* was written and presented to a group of Augustinian friars. At this point in his reforming work, Luther is still using the Catholic distinction between venial and mortal sins. Venial sins refer to those which are generally of less consequence while mortal are those who are deadly and are considered to push a person further away from God. Many of the theses deal with the reality that all sins—no matter how big or how small—are done out of disdain for God, and thus they are mortal or deadly. In this translation, we have chosen to change all uses of mortal to deadly.

[3]Ps. 7:9. The Bible verses which appear in the footnotes are ones that are not directly cited by Luther, but that he paraphrased. For this translation, those paraphrases have been replaced with the ESV translation.

[4]Acts 15:9

servant, Lord, for no living man is righteous in your presence. Thus speaks the Apostle Paul in Galatians 3. All who hope in works of the Law are under a curse. But the works of men are the works of the Law, and the curse is not upon lesser sins thus they are great or deadly sins. Thirdly, Romans 2:21 states, "You who teach, do not steal, do you steal?" Which Augustine explains, "Men are thieves in their desires, even if they judge others guilty of stealing."

4

THE WORKS OF GOD, THUS ALWAYS SEEM UGLY AND WICKED, NEVERTHELESS THEY ARE TRULY ETERNAL GAIN.

It is well known that the works of God are unattractive, according to Isaiah 53, "He is neither beautiful nor splendid," and 1 Samuel 2:6, "The Lord kills and makes alive, He stretches down to Sheol and restores it." This is understood to mean that the Lord humbles and terrifies us by means of the Law and the witness of our sins so that we appear in our own eyes as well as those of all men to be nothing, foolish, and wicked, for this is what we actually are. Insofar as we know and confess this, there is "no form or majesty" in us, but our life is buried in God (i.e. in the faithful trust of his mercy), having ourselves nothing except sin, foolishness, death, and hell. Thus the Apostle Paul pronounces in 2 Corinthians 6:9–10, "As unknown, and yet well known; as dying, and behold, we live." And this is what Isaiah 28 calls the "alien work" of God "to work his work" (that is, He humbles us, making us give up hope, so that in His mercy we are exalted, creating hope in us), just as Habakkuk 3:2 states, "In wrath remember mercy." Therefore man is so displeased with all his works; that he sees no beauty, but only his depravity. Indeed, he also does those things (of God) which seem foolish and ugly to others.

However, this disgrace, comes into us when God punishes and also when we accuse ourselves, as 1 Corinthians 11:31 says, "But if we judged ourselves truly, we would not be judged." Deuteronomy 32:36 also states, "For the LORD will vindicate his people and have compassion on his servants." In this way, the ugly works of God which are done in us, that is, those which are humble and fearing, are truly eternal, for humility and fear of God are in every way gained.

5 ══════════════════════════════════

THOSE WORKS OF MAN WHICH ARE CRIMES ARE NOT PART OF THE CATEGORY OF DEADLY SINS. WHEN SPEAKING ABOUT DEADLY SINS, I AM TALKING ABOUT THOSE WHICH APPEAR OUTWARDLY GOOD AND BENEFICIAL.

For instance, these are crimes which all men are able to identify: adultery, theft, murder, and deception. But deadly sins are those which appear good but in actuality are the result of a wicked tree bearing wicked fruit. Augustine affirms this in Book 4 of *Against Julian*.

6 ═══════════════════════════════════════

THE WORKS OF GOD, IN PARTICULAR, THOSE WHICH ARE DONE THROUGH MEN, ARE NOT DONE APART FROM SIN.

We read in Ecclesiastes 7, "Surely there is not a righteous man on earth who does good and never sins." From this, some say the justified man sins, but not when he is doing good works. They should be refuted saying, if that is what the text wanted to communicate, then why be superfluous with its words? Or does the Holy Spirit delight in overabundant and foolish ramblings? For this purpose could have been thoroughly expressed by the following: "There is not a righteous man on earth who never sins." Why add, "who does good," as if there are other persons who do evil and are righteous? For no one except a justified man does good. Where, however, he speaks of sins outside the realm of good works he speaks thus, "For the righteous falls seven times."[5] Here he does not say: A righteous man falls seven times daily while doing good. This is a good analogy: When someone cuts with a rusty and jagged ax, even though the carver is a good craftsman, the hatchet leaves bad, misplaced, and deformed cuts. So too, this is what it is like when God works through us.

---

[5]Prov. 24:16

7

THE WORKS OF THE JUSTIFIED ARE DEADLY SINS UNLESS THE JUSTIFIED THEMSELVES DREAD THEM TO BE DEADLY SINS OUT OF DEVOUT FEAR OF GOD.

This is clear from Thesis 4 of this work. Relying on works, which we ought to do out of fear, is the same thing as giving oneself glory and taking it away from God, to whom fear is owed in every work. For it is completely wrong to please, enjoy, and adore oneself and his works as an idol. Again whoever confidently trusts in all his works without fear of God acts like this. For if he possessed fear, he would not be confident, and for this reason he would not be satisfied with himself, but rather, he would have satisfaction in God.

Secondly, it is clear from the words of the Psalmist, "Enter not into judgment with your servant,"[6] and "I said, 'I will confess my transgressions to the LORD,'"[7] etc. It is clear that these are not venial sins because these verses proclaim that confession and repentance are not necessary for venial sins. If, they are deadly sins and "all the saints intercede for them," as it is stated in the same place, then the works of the saints are deadly sins. But the works of saints are good works, which are not meritorious apart from their fear and humble confession.

---

[6]Ps. 143:2
[7]Ps. 32:5

Thirdly, it is clear from the Lord's Prayer, "Forgive us our debts." This is the prayer of the saints, therefore those debts for which they pray become good works. But that these are deadly sins is clear from the following verse, "but if you do not forgive others their trespasses, neither will your Father forgive your trespasses." Take note that these sins are so great that they are damnable and unforgiven, unless the saints pray sincerely and actually forgive others.

Fourth and lastly, it is clear from Revelation 21:27, "But nothing unclean will ever enter it," that is the Kingdom of Heaven. But anything that prevents entrance into the kingdom of heaven is a deadly sin (Otherwise there would be another definition of deadly sin). However, small[8] sin prevents entrance because it pollutes the soul and cannot stand in the kingdom of heaven.

8

THE WORKS OF MAN ARE ALL THE MORE DEADLY WHEN THEY ARE DONE WITHOUT FEAR AND ARE ALIGNED WITH UNRESTRAINED AND EVIL SELF-SECURITY.

It is clear what necessarily follows this statement. For where there is no fear there is no humility. Where there is no humility there is arrogance, and where there is arrogance there lies the fury and judgment of God, "for God opposes

---

[8]venial

the proud."[9] Indeed, if pride ceased to exist there would be no sin anywhere.

9

SAYING THAT WORKS APART FROM CHRIST ARE DEAD, BUT NOT DEADLY, LOOKS LIKE A DANGEROUS TURN FROM THE FEAR OF GOD.

It is in this way that men become secure and therefore arrogant, which is dangerous. For in such a way, God is robbed of the glory which is owed to Him and it is scattered to others. With all zeal and quickness, one should strive to give Him glory; the sooner the better. Therefore, Scripture warns us, "Do not delay being converted to the Lord."[10] For whoever steals God's glory offends Him, how much greater does he offend who goes on stealing glory from Him and does it proudly. But whoever is not in Christ, or rejects Him, steals glory from Him. This is well known.

[9]Prov. 3:34; James 4:6
[10]Sir. 5:8

10

FURTHER, IT IS HARD TO UNDERSTAND HOW A WORK COULD BE DEAD AND ALSO NOT A HARMFUL AND DEATH-BEARING SIN.[11]

I will demonstrate this proof in the following way: Scripture does not contain a reference of dead things acting like this, stating that something could be at the same time dead and not death bearing.[12] Furthermore, the grammar, which calls "dead" a stronger word than "mortal" does not suggest this either. Grammarians call that which brings death a deadly work. To be sure, a "dead" work is not one that has been killed, but one that is not alive. But what is not alive displeases God, in Proverbs 15:8, "The sacrifice of the wicked is an abomination to the Lord."

Secondly, to some extent the will must navigate the road littered with dead works. This means, it must either love or despise them. However, the will is not able to hate dead works because it is evil. Therefore the will loves them and in so doing loves a dead thing. In that act itself, the will draws towards an evil work against God to whom it owes love and honor in this and in every other work.

---

[11]mortuum
[12]mortuum

11

SHAMELESSNESS CANNOT BE AVOIDED OR TRUE HOPE BE PRESENT UNLESS JUDGMENT AND CON-DEMNATION ARE FEARED IN EVERY WORK.

This is present from Thesis 4. Because it is impossible to trust in God unless one has let go of trust in created things and knows that nothing is of benefit to oneself short of God. Since there is no one who holds this pure hope, as we stated above, and since we still put some trust in created things, it is clear that on account of such lust in all things, we must fear the judgment of God. And this arrogance must be avoided, not only in the work, but in the affections also, that is, because it should displease us to have trusting faith in created things.

12

BEFORE GOD, SINS ARE TRULY OF LESS CONSE-QUENCE[13] WHEN THEY ARE FEARED AS DEADLY BY MEN.

This has been clearly laid out by what was said before. For as much as we accuse ourselves, all the more God justifies us, "Confess your misdeed so that you will be justified,"[14] and

---

[13]little sins or venial
[14]Is. 43:26

according to another, "Incline not my heart to any evil, to busy myself with wicked deeds."[15]

13

AFTER THE FALL, FREE WILL EXISTS ONLY AS A CONCEPT, AND AS LONG AS IT ACTS IN ACCORDANCE WITH ITSELF, COMMITS A DEADLY SIN.

The first part is apparent, for the will is a prisoner and slave to sin. In this way the will is not nothing, but it is not free with the exception that it does evil. John 8 states, "Everyone who commits sin is a slave to sin." "So if the Son makes you free, you will be free indeed."[16] For this reason, St. Augustine says in the book, *On the Spirit and the Letter,* "Without grace, free will has no power except the power to sin;" And in Book 2 of *Against Julian*, "You say the will is free, but in reality it is a slave," this follows in other writings.

The second part is made known by what was said above and from the verse in Hosea 13, "Israel, you are bringing misfortune upon yourself, for your salvation is alone with me." There are also other examples.

---

[15]Ps. 141:4
[16]John 8:36

14

AFTER THE FALL, FREE WILL ONLY HAS THE POWER TO PASSIVELY DO GOOD, BUT IT IS ALWAYS ABLE TO ACTIVELY DO EVIL.

Just as a dead man can only come to life passively, that same man as long as he lives, can bring himself to death actively. Moreover, free will is dead, this is revealed by the dead whom the Lord has lifted up. The holy teachers of the church say this as well. For example, St. Augustine comes to the same conclusion in his various writings, especially *Against the Pelagians*.

15

FURTHER STILL, FREE WILL COULD NOT REMAIN IN A STATE OF INNOCENCE, MUCH LESS ACTIVELY DO GOOD, BUT THE WILL IS ONLY ABLE TO DO GOOD PASSIVELY.

The Master of the Sentences,[17] quoting Augustine, states, "By these testimonies it is abundantly revealed that man received righteousness and a good will at creation, and also the things necessary to remain in that nature, or else it would seem that

---

[17]Peter Lombard was a scholastic Bishop and theologian. Lombard is most well known for his *Libri Quatuor Sententiarum* or *Four Books of Sentences*. This volume was used as the standard textbook for theological education spanning nearly four centuries. While Luther respected Lombard, he also understood that much of the theological error of his time was in part due to semi-Pelagian writings included within *The Sentences*.

he had not fallen on account of his own fault." Lombard talks about the active ability of the will in a way that is obviously contrary to Augustine in his book *Reprimand and Grace*, where it states, "He received the power to act, if he desired, but he did not have the will to actually utilize the power to act." By "power to act" he understands the passive ability, and by will to actually utilize, the active ability.

The second portion of this thesis, is abundantly clear from the earlier instruction of the Master.

16

THE PERSON WHO THINKS THAT BY DOING WHAT IS IN HIM,[18] HE CAN WILLINGLY MAKE HIMSELF MOVE TOWARD GRACE, ADDS SIN TO SIN IN SUCH A WAY THAT HE BECOMES TWICE AS GUILTY.

---

[18]The text here presents a variation of the phrase *facere quod in se est*, which literally translates as "to do what is in oneself" meaning "do your best." In Scholastic theology, this phrase was often used in regards to grace and salvation as in, "do your best and God will do the rest." By the time of the *Heidelberg Disputation*, Luther understood this key component of medieval theology to be a watered down version of works-righteousness and self justification. Not only did this concept turn the Gospel into something which must be earned, but it made it impossible for the believer to know whether he or she had actually done their best. The *Heidelberg Disputation* is a full blown attack against this logic. It returns to Scripture in order to show that "what is in oneself" is not good but wholly corrupted by sin. Humanity has no *best* to offer God; we must wholly trust in the work of Christ *extra nos,* that is outside of ourselves.

Because of what was said before, the following is clear: When a person is doing what is in him, he sins and wholly seeks himself. But if he believes that through sin he could be suitable to receive or obtain grace, he would add arrogant stubbornness to his sin and not believe that sin is sin and evil is evil, which is an even greater sin. As Jeremiah 2:13 says, "for my people have committed two evils: they have forsaken me, the fountain of living waters, and hewed out cisterns for themselves, broken cisterns that can hold no water." That is, on account of sin they are far away from me and yet they presume to do good by themselves.

Now you ask: What can we do? Should we walk calmly because we can do nothing except sin? I would answer: By no means. But, having heard these proofs, fall down and pray for grace and transfer your hope from yourself to Christ in Whom lies our salvation, life, and resurrection. Because we have been taught these things and because the Law makes sin known so that, in knowing sin, one might beg and receive grace.[19] Thus God "gives grace to the humble,"[20] and "whoever humbles himself will be exalted."[21] The Law humbles; grace lifts up. The Law brings about fear and wrath; grace brings about hope and mercy. Through the Law comes knowledge of sin.[22] Moreover, by the knowledge of sin, humility is acquired and through

---

[19]The word used for "receive or obtain" here, *impetretur,* can only be translated in this way after verbs of asking or entreaty, meaning that the reception is in no part due to the asker but only due to the grace of the giver.

[20]1 Peter 5:5

[21]Matt. 23:12

[22]Rom. 3:20

humility grace is gained. Thus God's alien work brings out a work which is His very own: that is He brings forth the sinner that He might make him just.

17

NOR IS SPEAKING LIKE THIS A REASON TO BE HOPELESS, BUT CAUSES ONE TO BE HUMBLED AND SEEK AFTER THE GRACE OF CHRIST.

This is clear from what has been said, for, according to the Gospel, the kingdom of heaven is given to little children and the humble,[23] and Christ loves them. Those who do not recognize that they are damnable and awful-smelling sinners cannot be humble. However, sin cannot be known except through the Law. Clearly, when we are called sinners it is not despair, but rather hope, which is preached. Preaching about sin is preparation for grace, or even more importantly such preaching creates knowledge of sin and faith. For example desiring grace rises up after knowledge of sin has been created. A sick person seeks treatment when he recognizes how severe his illness is. In the same way, it does not produce despair or death when a sick person is told about the danger of his illness, but instead urges him to seek medical treatment. To say that we are nothing and always sin when we do what is in us is not hopeless (unless we are stupid); rather, it makes one focus on the grace of our Lord Jesus Christ.

---

[23]Mark 10:14

18 ════════════════════════════════════

IT IS CERTAIN THAT MAN MUST GIVE UP ALL HOPE IN HIS OWN ABILITY BEFORE HE IS ABLE TO RECEIVE THE GRACE OF CHRIST.

The law desires that man give up hope in himself, for it leads him to hell and makes him miserable and shows him that he is a sinner in all of his works. The Apostle Paul does this in Romans 2 and 3:9, where he says, "I have already charged that all men are under the power of sin." However, he who does what is within him and believes that he is as a result doing good does not consider himself worthless, nor does he give up on his own strength. Indeed, he is so self-consumed that he depends on his own strength to get closer to grace.

19 ════════════════════════════════════

THAT PERSON IS NOT WORTHY TO BE CALLED A THEOLOGIAN WHO THINKS THE INVISIBLE THINGS OF GOD ARE OBSERVABLE FROM EVENTS WHICH HAVE ACTUALLY HAPPENED (ROM. 1:20; 1 COR. 1:21-25).

This is clear from those who were theologians and yet were still called fools by the Apostle Paul in Romans 1. Additionally, the invisible things of God are virtue, godliness, wisdom, justice, goodness, and so forth. The knowledge of all these things does not make one worthy or wise.

20

CONVERSELY, A PERSON IS WORTHY OF BEING CALLED A THEOLOGIAN WHO UNDERSTANDS THE VISIBLE AND ORDERED THINGS OF GOD AFTER FIXING HIS SIGHT ON THE PASSION AND CROSS OF CHRIST.

The observable and visible things of God, that is His humanity, weakness, and foolishness, are the opposite of the invisible. The Apostle Paul in 1 Corinthians 1:25 calls them the weakness and foolishness of God. Because by works men abused the knowledge of God, to the contrary, God desired to be known in suffering, and to reject wisdom of invisible things by means of the wisdom of visible things, so that those who did not cling to God as present in his works should cling to Him as He is hidden in His suffering. As the Apostle Paul says in 1 Corinthians 1:21, "For since, in the wisdom of God, the world did not know God through wisdom, it pleased God through the folly of what we preach to save those who believe." Therefore, it is not enough for anyone, and it has no benefit to know God in glory and majesty, unless that person knows Him in the humility and shame of the cross. Thus God destroys the wisdom of the wise, as Isaiah 45:15 states, "Truly, thou art a God who hides Himself."

So, also, in John 14:8, where Philip spoke about the theology of glory: "Show us the Father." Christ quickly corrected his wandering thought about seeking God elsewhere and led him back to Himself, saying, "Philip, he who has seen me has seen the Father."[24] For this reason, true theology and knowledge of God are in Christ crucified, as it is also says in John 10, "No one comes to the Father, except by me." "I am the door,"[25] and so on and so forth.

21

A THEOLOGIAN OF GLORY SAYS THAT EVIL IS GOOD AND GOOD IS EVIL. A THEOLOGIAN OF THE CROSS SAYS THAT A THING IS WHAT IT ACTUALLY IS.

This is clear: He who disregards Christ disregards God hidden in suffering. For this reason the theologian of glory prefers works to suffering, glory to the cross, strength to weakness, wisdom to folly, and, in general, good to evil. These are whom the Apostle Paul calls "enemies of the cross of Christ,"[26] for they hate the cross and suffering and love works and their glory. This is why theologians of glory call the good of the cross evil and the evil of a work good. God can only be found in suffering and the cross. As was said before, the allies of the cross say that the cross is good and works are evil, for through the cross, works are torn down and with them the Old Adam, who is constructed by works, is crucified. In fact, it is impossible for a person not to be inflated by his good works who has not first been

---

[24]John 14:9
[25]John 10:9
[26]Phil. 3:18

deflated and torn down by suffering and evil, that is until he knows that he is worthless and that his works are not his but are God's.

22

THAT PARTICULAR WISDOM WHICH USES WORKS TO INTERPRET THE INVISIBLE THINGS OF GOD ENTIRELY INFLATES, BLINDS, AND HARDENS.

This has already been said since men disregard the cross and hate it, they necessarily love the opposite, namely, wisdom, glory, power, etc. Therefore they become all the more blind and hard by such great love, for it is impossible for lust to be satisfied by the acquisition of the things which it desires. This just like the love of money which grows in proportion to the increase of wealth itself, so when the soul loses its substance,[27] it becomes thirstier and drinks more, as the poet says: "The more water they drink, the more they thirst for it." The same thought is expressed in Ecclesiastes 1:8: "The eye is not satisfied with seeing, nor the ear filled with hearing." This is true for all desires.

So also lust for knowledge is not satisfied by the acquisition of wisdom but is that much more aroused. Likewise, lust for glory is not satisfied by the acquisition of glory, nor is the lust for control satisfied by power and authority, nor is the desire for praise satisfied by praise, and so on, as Christ

---

[27] The word used here is *hydropisis* referring to the medical condition of dropsy which causes the loss of vital liquids.

demonstrates in John 4:13, where He declares, "Everyone who drinks of this water will thirst again."

So it stands that lust cannot be cured by satisfaction, but by extinguishing it. In other words, he whoever wishes to become wise does not seek wisdom by rushing toward it but becomes a fool seeking to be returned to foolishness. Likewise, he who wants to have a lot of power, honor, pleasure, and satisfaction in all things must run away rather than seek power, honor, pleasure, and satisfaction in all things. This is the wisdom which is idiotic to the world.

23

THE LAW WORKS THE WRATH OF GOD,[28] LAYS SLAUGHTER, CURSES, ACCUSES, JUDGES, AND CONDEMNS EVERYTHING THAT IS NOT IN CHRIST.

Thus Galatians 3:13 states, "Christ redeemed us from the curse of the law," and "For all who rely on works of the law are under the curse,"[29] and Romans 4:15, "For the law brings wrath," and Romans 7:10, "The very commandment which promised life proved to be the death of me," Romans 2:12, "All who have sinned without the law will also perish without law." Therefore whoever brags as if he were wise and educated in the Law brags about his confusion, being cursed, the wrath of God, and death. As Romans 2:23 puts it, "You who boast in the law."

---

[28]Rom. 4:15
[29]Gal. 3:10

24

YET WISDOM IS NOT ITSELF EVIL, NOR SHOULD THE LAW BE AVOIDED, BUT WITHOUT THE THEOLOGY OF THE CROSS, MAN MISUSES THE GREATEST THINGS AS IF THEY WERE THE WORST THINGS.

Indeed the Law is holy,[30] every gift of God is good,[31] and every-thing created is very good, as in Genesis 1:31. But, as stated above, whoever has not been torn down and driven back to nothingness through the cross and suffering, takes the credit for good works and wisdom and for himself while also not giving credit to God. And so he abuses and violates the gifts of God.

Whoever has been emptied[32] by suffering recognizes that he no longer works but God works and does all things in him. So whether or not works actually happen in him does not matter. He does not brag if he does good works, nor is he worried if God does not do good works through him. For he knows that it is enough for him to suffer and be torn down by the cross with the result that he is brought to nothingness. It is this that Christ says in John 3:7, "You must be born anew." To be born anew, one must first die and then be resurrected with the Son of Man. It is taught that to die means to experience death first hand.

---

[30]Rom. 7:12

[31]1 Tim. 4:4

[32]Phil. 2:7

25

HE IS NOT JUSTIFIED WHO DOES MANY WORKS, BUT HE WHO, WITHOUT WORK, BELIEVES MUCH IN CHRIST.

For the righteousness of God is not acquired by constantly repeated action, which is what Aristotle taught, but righteousness is poured out by faith, for "The righteous shall live by faith."[33] And, "for with the heart one believes and is justified."[34] I want the words "without work" understood like this: Not that the one who is justified does nothing, but that his works do not justify him. In fact his justification produces works. For grace and faith are poured out without our works and works follow after they are poured out. Thus Romans 3:20 and 28 state, "For by works of the law no human being will be justified in his sight" and, "For we hold that one is justified by faith apart from works of the law." In other words, works contribute nothing toward justification.

Therefore man knows that works which he does through faith are not his but God's. For this reason, he does not strive to be justified or glorified through them, but seeks God. His justification by faith in Christ is enough for him. Christ is his wisdom, righteousness, etc., as 1 Corinthians 1:30 says, he himself becomes a vessel and instrument for Christ.

---

[33]Rom. 1:17
[34]Rom. 10:10

26

THE LAW SAYS, DO THIS, AND IT IS NEVER DONE. GRACE SAYS, BELIEVE IN THIS, AND ALL THINGS ARE ALREADY DONE.

The first clause is clear from what the Apostle Paul says and his interpreter, St. Augustine, also confirms in many works. And it has been said many times in the above theses that the Law works wrath and keeps all men under the curse. The second clause is clear from the same texts, for faith justifies. And according to Augustine, the Law commands that which faith delivers. For Christ is in us through faith, in fact, He is one with us. Christ is just and has fulfilled all the commandments of God, therefore on account of Him, we also fulfill everything on the condition that He has crafted our fulfillment through faith.

27

ACTUALLY ONE SHOULD CALL THE WORK OF CHRIST AN ACTIVELY FUNCTIONING WORK[35] AND OUR WORK IS A COMPLETED WORK,[36] AND THUS A COMPLETED WORK WHICH IS PLEASING TO GOD BY THE GRACE OF CHRIST'S ACTIVE WORK.

Since Christ lives in us on account of faith, so He moves us through the living faith in His work to do good works.

[35] *Operans*
[36] *Operatum*

For the works which He completes are the fulfillment of the commandments which God has given us through faith, and when we look at them we are moved to imitate them. This is what the Apostle Paul says, "Therefore be imitators of God, as beloved children."[37] Therefore merciful works are brought about by those ones which saved us, as St. Gregory says: "Every one of Christ's actions is instruction for us, in fact it is a driving force." If His action is in us then it lives by faith, for it vigorously drives us closer to Him. "Draw me after you, let us make haste" toward the fragrance "of your anointing oils,"[38] that is, your works.

28

THE LOVE OF GOD DOES NOT FIND, BUT CREATES, THAT WHICH IS LOVABLE. THE LOVE OF MAN IS MADE UP OF THOSE THINGS WHICH IT LOVES.

The second clause is well known and held in common by all philosophers and theologians because the object is the cause of love. Likewise, Aristotle proposes that all the soul's power is passive and material and active only by receiving something. Thus Aristotle's philosophy reveals itself to be contrary to theology because in all things it desires to indulge its nature and receives rather than imparts goodness. The first clause is clear because the love of God which lives in man loves sinners, wicked people, fools, and cowards with the

---

[37]Eph. 5:1
[38]Song 1:4,3

result that it makes them righteous, good, wise, and brave. Rather than seeking its own goodness, the love of God pours out and bestows goodness. Therefore sinners are lovable because they are loved; they are not loved because they are actually lovable by nature. For this reason the love of man runs away from sinners and evil persons. Thus Christ says, "For I came not to call the righteous, but sinners."[39]

This is the love of the cross, and that which is produced by the cross, which turns towards the direction where it cannot find the goodness in which it delights, but where it may transfer goodness onto the wicked and the destitute. The Apostle Paul states, "It is more blessed to give than to receive,"[40] Hence Psalms 41:1 declares, "Blessed is he who considers the poor," for the intellect by nature cannot understand an object which does not actually exist, that is the poor and needy, but only an object which does exist, that is the truth and goodness. Therefore it judges according to appearance, takes hold of human character, and judges according to things which are obvious, etc.

---

[39]Matt. 9:13
[40]Acts 20:35

Theses 1 & 2

THE TRUTH THAT
THE LAW IS GOOD

CALEB KEITH

❝ ————————————————————————

(1) The Law of God, which is the most beneficial doctrine of life, is not able to advance man toward righteousness but rather stands against him. (2) Much less could the work of men, that is to say even works which are done over and over again with the help of natural law, move someone toward righteousness.

The first thing to note about the *Heidelberg Disputation* is that the theses do not stand alone, but rather work together in pairs or groups to drive home a particular point. In this way, Theses 1 and 2 function as a unit describing the goodness of God's Law while simultaneously explaining how sinners misuse this good gift. Luther holds nothing back in the introductory article of this Disputation. In part, this is because he is defending the principles which led him to post the 95 Theses. You can imagine that Luther has been under a lot of criticism for the six months between these two disputations. Now, he is taking the opportunity to approach fellow friars and clergy from the Augustinian Order with a clear presentation of the doctrine which he saw revealed in Scripture.

The first thesis lays the foundation for his entire disputation with the reality that God's Law is powerful, efficacious, and works to our utmost benefit. This is something to which all late medieval theologians would have ascribed. Yet while opening up with a point of agreement, Luther also indicates where the doctrine of the Law has been misused. Luther sees that the Law has been turned into a checklist of saving works. But Scripture tells a different story: the Law is perfectly beneficial, but its benefit is not the ability to save sinners. In fact, it is the exact opposite. The Law is the greatest good in this life because it relentlessly accuses the sinner even when his actions seem naturally or civilly good. Luther's accusation removes the works of the sinner from the salvation equation, leaving room for Christ alone.

In Thesis 2, Luther recognizes that most people appear to do good regularly in their lives. Most of us could claim to be "good people" perhaps giving back to charity or offering a kind word here or there to our neighbor. However, following the Law is not simply about external actions but about human nature, the will, and the heart. In reality, this apparent good is void of true righteousness. It is not only our works which are wicked but our hearts and our minds, something Luther will address more thoroughly later in the Disputation.

Luther has often been accused of turning the Law into something bad which ought to be avoided. This is because Luther emphasizes the accusing and killing power the Law has over sinners. However, this accusation is simply untrue: the Law is praised and highly regarded by both Luther and later Lutheran teaching. The Law is part of God's redemptive plan yet it is not the redeemer. Luther clearly and consistently distinguishes the attributes of the Law—that which is good, perfect and holy—with the purpose of the Law. The Law, he asserts, was not meant to save but rather to turn the sinner away from relying on himself for salvation and towards the works of God. This contrast between the good works of God and the wickedness of men is at the core of every thesis. The Law is a warrior sent to strike down proud sinners; it paves the way for Christ who by His death and resurrection brings life to those who have been struck dead by the Law on account of their sin.

The Theology of the Cross begins with the Law because this doctrine was thoroughly misunderstood by the semi-Pelagian teaching of Luther's time. The Law reveals the depths of our sin and thus, our great need for a mediator in the presence of the Almighty. The Law simultaneously elevates the goodness of God as it unmasks the wickedness of man, even when we think we are at our best. In light of these truths, our only hope for salvation is Jesus Christ who suffered the consequences of sin and death that we might be freed and have eternal life. Theses 1 and 2 of the *Heidelberg Disputation* start the journey toward a Cross-centered approach to Christian doctrine.

Theses 3 & 4

THE INVERTED WAY OF JESUS

DAN VAN VOORHIS

"

(3) Even though the works of man always seem to be beautiful and good, they are nevertheless demonstrably deadly sins. (4) The works of God, thus always seem ugly and wicked, nevertheless, they are truly eternal gain.

Greeks seek wisdom, Jews seek a sign, and modern Christians seem to like big monuments and buildings. Our folly in doing so has caught the attention of everyone since Babel to the present day, always with a predictable ending. Consider Percy Bysshe Shelley's famous 19th-century ode to the great king Ozymandias. It is unlikely that Shelley was familiar with Luther's theology of the cross, but his poem uses the same irony and inverted logic. "Look on my Works, ye Mighty, and Despair!" reads the inscription on the great monument to the once feared king. However, we soon learn that this king is long since dead, and this inscription we read remains on only a fragment of the monument, destroyed and in rubble. The once great Ozymandias and his monument are now all but forgotten. Luther similarly "praises" the works of man as mighty, only to then flip the tables in order to magnify the grace of God.

In the *Heidelberg Disputation*, Luther presents the Gospel which crushes the mighty and proud and elevates the humble and lowly. The message in Theses 3 and 4 of the *Heidelberg Disputation* is this: Be careful praising the accomplishments of man while missing the hidden, and sometimes despised, works of God. Even the best of our works that we call beautiful and good pale in comparison to the mighty works of God. Luther further suggests that boasting in these works is deadly. Yet each of us continues to build and worship idols.

Take for instance the monuments we have built for our earthly gods. The great pyramid alone has over two million stones weighing as much as fifteen tons each. Many more millions of slaves were told that god's only plan for their life was to lug stones for a foreign king and then die. Sometimes our man-made, impressive gods end up acting like tyrants. The Hanging Gardens of Babylon exalted themselves over nature as a man-made oasis in a desert, built with the express intent of establishing hierarchy and lording it over the people. The Washington Monument took over twenty years, a civil war, and the weight of a nation, to finally hoist the world's tallest obelisk in the beltway skyline. In the very top of the monument is an inscription praising God, but certainly, at some point, visions of Babel crossed their minds. The God of the Bible is not easily impressed with monuments. Yahweh is not into looks (despite the curiously well-coifed, sun-kissed tan Jesus of some Bibles). In fact, if we want to know anything about the appearance of Jesus, consider this description given by the prophet Isaiah:

**He had no beauty or majesty to attract us to him,
nothing in his appearance that we should desire him.**

> **He was despised and forsaken of men**
> **A Man of sorrows and acquainted with grief;**
> **And like one from whom men hide their face**
> **He was despised and we did not esteem him (Is. 53:2–3)**

This deformed yet divine servant will be God's mouthpiece. And as all advertisers know, if you don't have a pretty product, you had better have a really good product. The theology of the cross, a Jesus-centered religion, put all its weight in the message. Our God is not like a Marvel superhero, but rather like one who after finding a treasure hidden in a field, goes and sells all that he has, and buys that field. Our God looks forsaken, foolish, and even irresponsible.

The theology of the cross inverts our obelisks reaching to heaven and sends heaven down to earth, albeit, not in the kind of package you probably expected. We want our works to matter, and so we make them bigger. The irony is that as we are building these bigger and more attractive, God inverts the way of the world in Jesus. St. Paul famously highlights this in a great early exploration of the theology of the cross:

> **Who, though he was in the form of God, did not count equality with God a thing to be grasped, but emptied himself, by taking the form of a servant, being born in the likeness of men. And being found in human form, he humbled himself by becoming obedient to the point of death, even death on a cross. Therefore God has highly exalted him and bestowed on him the name that is above every name, so that at the name of Jesus every knee should bow, in heaven and on earth and under the earth, and every**

tongue confess that Jesus Christ is Lord, to the glory of God the Father. (Phil. 2:6-11)

It is this emptying and humbling that turns the wisdom of this world on its head. God has become man and victory comes through His death. It was the message, of a logic-of-the-world, turned upside down, summarized in the *Heidelberg Disputation.* From Paul to Luther, we are taught to let all the other gods, and theologies, and spiritual narratives impress with their size and stature. Greeks seek wisdom, Jews seek a sign, but despite all the magnificent buildings, and burial places and monuments, our God still prefers to be found in the green wood of the manger and the old, splintered wood of the Roman cross.

Theses 5 & 6

THE DEADLY SIN IN ALL OF US

KELSI KLEMBARA

"

> **(5) Those works of man which are crimes are not part of the category of deadly sins. When speaking about deadly sins, I am talking about those which appear outwardly good and beneficial. (6) The works of God, in particular, those which are done through men, are not done apart from sin.**

I am the queen of "good works." I grew up doing my chores early so I could find extra to-do's around the house. I never missed curfew. I received straight As. I volunteered more during my first two years of college than I took credited hours of classes. My first job out of college was with a non-profit (which also meant I had to work two other jobs to support myself). I curse only on occasion, and to my mother's delight, I have no tattoos. You get the idea. I am just the type of self-righteous person who finds it easy to put my trust in the bounty of my perceived goodness, and therefore, I am just the type of person Luther addresses in Theses 5 and 6 of his *Heidelberg Disputation*.

Luther has already laid out the beginnings of his argument in the preceding theses: the Law of God does not have the power to get you where you want to be, virtuous works done in repetitious fashion have no innate bearing on righteousness, and furthermore, such works are deadly. So we dress our achievements up in beautiful adornments to hide their fatality, and at the same time, we fling God's works aside as if they were disgusting garbage. Before moving on too quickly, Luther takes a little aside in Thesis 5 and 6 to make sure He is extremely clear on one thing: none of us, not the good works queens and kings, the righteous and redeemed, nor the theologically savvy reading this right now, none of us can avoid deadly sin in this life.

Obvious crimes are not what Luther's after. Adultery, theft, murder, and lies: these sins do not betray the sinful conscience, but instead, they expose it. A murderer knows he is culpable, the adulteress has no qualms about her purity, and everyone knows you should not steal what is not yours to take. Any sane person understands there is nothing good about a crime. Yet what can we say about the sins we refuse to admit, all of which trace back to a lack of faith in Christ? Luther levels the playing field by making this seemingly obvious point: No longer can the righteous put herself on a pedestal above the criminal. In fact, the sins of the criminal don't even fit the same definition as hers—all of which appear beautiful and picturesque yet are killing her from the inside.

Our lives are inundated with the beautiful and pictur-esque. "Live longer, happier lives through health, wealth, and a dose of thoughtful charity," is our zeitgeist. And the longer we live, the less we think about death. Death is such a dreary topic, anyway, it's always certain to dampen the mood! So we push for more comfort, less suffering, and convince ourselves that no one deserves pain and hardship. No one deserves to die, and if no one deserves death, then no one is sinful.

This is why what appears to be good is the most deadly. Our smallish and constant attempts to save ourselves and the world around us trick us into thinking we are capable of eternal salvation. And thus, our works keep us from trusting in the only One who can indeed deliver eternal life. Any sin, no matter how inconsequential, cuts us off from our Creator and our true savior. "Your iniquities have separated you from your God; your sins have hidden his face from you, so that he will not hear" (Is. 59:2). The small sins of our good works: pride, self-righteousness, "godliness," and charity are the sins we least expect to have lasting consequences; in fact, we rarely view them as sins at all! Yet generation after generation, here is where we continue to find ourselves most deceived, and most cut off from the God of the universe. These little sins expose the very nature of sin: the constant battle we fight with God to try and save ourselves rather than let Him save us.

Not only are these sins the most deadly, but they are the sins we all have. We cannot escape them, we cannot deny them, even when, as Thesis 6 states, God works through us despite them. Here, Luther drives home the point that no matter how and when God chooses to use us, praise and honor goes solely to Him. We can't take the credit: He is the master craftsman, and we are the rusty ax, He is the artist, and we are the old and dirty paintbrush. Don't doubt that good can be done through you, but do doubt your ability to contribute anything other than sin and resistance.

Our sin is not just that thin layer of dust plaguing your furniture—it is much more pervasive. We assume the harder we work to appear good, the less sinful we will become. Scrub hard enough and often enough and that veneer of dust will hardly be noticeable. The good will outweigh the bad, the good works queens of the world will finally triumph.

Unfortunately, neither Scripture nor experience shows this to be the case. On our own, in our pervasive sin, we are separated from God and wholly unrighteous. No amount of chores, exercise, or studying can change our ontology. Seeking to observe and quantify our goodness based on works is a fatal task because not even the jagged good done by God through us is free from sin. In this fallen and broken world, the righteous remain *simul iustus et peccator*, simultaneously fully righteous and fully sinner. Luther bases his proof of Thesis 6 on Ecclesiastes 7:20, "Surely there is not a righteous man on earth who does good and never sins." Can you imagine the panic in the room as Luther read these words? How then is one made righteous? Just as the minds of those Augustinian friars began to attempt to count up their goodness and reason themselves out of the category of sinners described by Luther, the piercing truth of God's law breaks in again. Be wary, righteous one, good works queen, self-sacrificial servant, self-help guru, for you cannot escape sin in this life.

I can imagine this panic because I've experienced it myself. Although oftentimes when I hear God's law, "You therefore must be perfect, as your heavenly Father is perfect," I may use these words to confirm my own self-righteousness and go about my business convinced I've fulfilled His commands (Matt. 5:48). Yet every once while, I realize how imperfect I truly am. Suddenly, I know that although I did my chores and more, my real motivation was always to receive praise from my parents. I can't hide behind my volunteer work because I am slapped in the face with how little I care for my neighbor if not for the recognition I receive from doing so. I know the only reason I don't have a tattoo is because I am afraid of the pain it would take to get one. The Law exposes the real me, the works queen without her crown: ugly, mortal, and desperate for righteousness. I need the type of righteousness that will save me from this failing body and failing world, *iustitia salutifera* or saving righteousness, not the type that will give me what I deserve, *iustitia distributiva.*[1] But from where can such righteousness come?

Only in Christ and by Christ have we, who are wholly sinful, been wholly justified. Our hope does not come from within; it comes from without. We are dying inside; our self-justifying works are killing us. Left to their own devices, these killing works would convince us we get what we deserve and what we deserve is happiness, health, and eternal life. We need a saving righteousness, won for us by a perfect life, death, and resurrection to break the spell. Our perfect God reminds us that what we truly deserve is death. But then in a miraculous turn, He does the dying for us and hands over eternal life. In Christ, we are daily killed and made alive. It's true His work appears deadly, perhaps the deadliest of all. Yet look closely and you'll see it is more beautiful than anything you've ever seen, for as dying, behold, we live (2 Cor. 6:9).

---

[1] Alister McGrath, *Luther's Theology of the Cross: Martin Luther's Theological Breakthrough,* 2nd ed. (Oxford: Blackwell Publishing Ltd., 2011), 136.

Theses 7 & 8

LET YOUR WORKS BE DAMNABLE

LARRY HUGHES

" ────────────────────────────────

(7) The works of the justified are mortal sins unless the justified themselves dread them to be mortal sins out of devout fear of God. (8) The works of man are all the more deadly when they are done without fear and are aligned with unrestrained and evil self-security.

In more than 500 years post-Reformation, no single work cuts through the noise and clatter pretending to be the Christian faith more than Martin Luther's *Heidelberg Disputation*. In 28 theological theses, Luther exposes the nature and structure of the only two theologies (or religions) that exist: the false way by which fallen man attempts to "save" himself, and the one, true salvation of God. Thesis 7 and 8, in particular, address the issues of trust and security both for the Christian and the non-Christian.

In Thesis 7, Luther addresses what the Christian's actual state-of-being is and is not after conversion. Christians stand palpably unholy, yet entirely holy on account of Christ's righteousness. This sinner/saint distinction is sometimes referred to as the "old Adam," or the reality that even Christians are still completely sinful in this life, and "new Adam," or the reality that Christians are also completely justified. Our holiness is on account of Christ alone—as the Prophet Jeremiah states, "In his days Judah will be saved, and Israel will dwell securely. And this is the name by which He will be called: The Lord [Christ] is our righteousness" (Jer. 23:6). Because we contribute nothing to this holiness, we must rely completely on God rather than on our own works.

The old Adam distrusts God and desires to be lord of his/her own destiny and salvation. We are glory-stealers, as Luther says. Suspicious of God and warring against Him, the sinner cannot help but to listen to the whisper of the Serpent and trust himself by relying on his best works. Man adores and relishes himself in good works in an attempt to be holy like God (Gen. 3:15). Behind every best and highest work is the desire to make oneself a god.

Luther carries this thought into Thesis 8: if the struggle to trust in one's own works still exists in the justified man, how much more will this be the case for the non-Christian. Here, he challenges our way of thinking about what is good and evil in an unfamiliar way. No person would argue that theft, murder, or other overt evils are righteous before God. Furthermore, all religions "do holy works" to either become more like their god or for the "glory of the deity worshipped." Man's dilemma is not the climb towards achieving perfectly good works. Rather, his problem is that good works done in pride, apart from fear of God, are always and completely damnable as sin.

Therefore, Luther establishes the human condition in two, and only two realities; the Christian (Thesis 7) and the unbeliever (Thesis 8). There is no third purgatorial state of "figuring out if one is a Christian." There are no levels of Christian holiness based on one's avoidance of sin or one's success at good works. The difference between the Christian and the non-Christian is not based on works or sins, but on where they place their security. Thesis 7 and 8 are not simply aimed at errant medieval Roman Catholicism. Rather, they address this same error of the object of faith wherever and whenever it freshly emerges in all times and places, including post-reformation Protestantism.

To understand their application to all Christendom, and not just medieval Roman Catholicism, one must understand what Rome meant by mortal and venial sin, and how Luther redefines these terms.

At the most basic level, all agree: mortal sin separates one from God's grace, and a venial sin does not. This medieval distinction arises out of a human desire to understand the ongoing presence of sin in the life of the Christian. Rome defined a mortal sin by its quality, magnitude, severity, and willful nature. If one's sin was willful or severe enough, it was mortal. If not, it was considered venial. Typically willful sexual sins, large crimes, and "unconquered" repetitive sins were mortal. Venial sins tended to be misdemeanors and accidental sins, although much gray area existed in between the two. Mortal sin meant spiritual death and separation from God while venial sins could generally be atoned for through acts penance.

This system left people unsure of their standing before God in several ways. When was a sin mortal or willful? When was penance needed and how much? And lastly, how could one truly know their good works outweighed their sins?

Today it would appear we have not moved far from Rome. Though Protestant Christians have ditched the terms "mortal" and "venial," we still find ourselves ranking our sins and our works from least to greatest. Which sins mean we have lost our salvation? What act reveals once and for all we were never elect? Which works can show we are saved or elect? Back and forth we go, weighing and measuring at every step. Before we know it, we find ourselves in the same purgatorial state-of-mind as the 16th-century laity. St. Paul's bold and certain faith seems, at best elusive, and at worst, entirely out of reach. Our use of these "holy metric systems" lays bare the true depths and reality of original sin: the exchange of faith in God for faith in oneself, or the disregard of humility before God in favor of the arrogance of self. Adam and Eve's original sin was more than just illegal action—it was complete distrust of God in an attempt to be like God.

This is why Luther decided to turn these words upside down. Luther's view is from the cross. If man's good works are in play anywhere in salvation's course, then what in the world is Jesus Christ doing living, suffering, dying and rising? Both the believer's and unbeliever's works alike are mortal, deadly sins if instead of being feared as such, they are praised for bringing righteousness and life. Good works are a very great, evil temptation if one does not fear them as such out of pious fear before God. When we fear trusting in good works, we assume we must put our trust somewhere outside of ourselves, namely, in Christ. Thus, Christ alone and His work on the cross is the sole hope of the Christian.

When the Christian appears before Christ's judgment seat to receive what is due for the good or evil they have done in the body (2 Cor. 5:10), they will not offer up to Christ their "good works" as opposed to their evil deeds. Rather, they will confess all that they have done is sin worthy of condemnation and cling solely to the mercy of that nail-driven hand. This is the pious fear of God—without any other support than in God's mercy and graciousness.

The Law deals a death blow to our religious projects that no other religion dares deliver, "By the works of the Law no flesh will be justified in His sight" (Rom. 3:20). And as a result of this great blow, the Gospel is always even more unexpected as God resurrects us with, "I forgive you on account of My Son, rise and enter into the kingdom of heaven good and faithful servant."

Theses 9 & 10

" ————————————————————————

(9) Saying that works apart from Christ are dead, but not deadly, looks like a dangerous turn from the fear of God. (10) Further, it is hard to understand how a work could be dead and also not a harmful and mortal sin.

If God gave out gold medals for good works, the prize would often go to people who never darken the doors of a church. Thomas, the atheist, because he has deep compassion for the homeless population, establishes a local shelter and soup kitchen where the poor can have a roof over the heads and a hot meal. Sandra, the agnostic, runs a local clinic that specializes in caring for those ensnared by addictions. Mohammed, a Muslim social worker, labors tirelessly to assist and free victims of sex trafficking. These people either deny God, question his existence, or reject the Trinity, yet they're committed to helping their neighbor, doing good, and protecting the unfortunate. They are, by society's standards, good people.

If Thomas, Sandra, and Mohammed sat down with you asked, "So, what do you, as a Christian, think of our good works?" what would you say? More specifically, what if they asked you, "What does your God think of our good works?" how would you respond?

Such questions take us into the heart of Theses 9–10 of the *Heidelberg Disputation*.

If we're operating with a sort of Common Sense theology, then this question is a no-brainer: God applauds all good works, no matter who does them. What does it matter if the doer is an atheist, Hindu, a religious "None", or Mother Teresa? If the work is good, it's good—plain and simple. Don't overthink this. Who really cares what the person believes? What matters is the deed itself. God, who is good, rejoices to see others do good. He doesn't stop to ask what's in their heart before He approves of what their hands accomplish. So speaks the common sense theologian.

If we put ourselves into the shoes of 16th-century scholastic theologians (whom Luther was addressing), the matter is a bit more tangled. They would insist that the works of unbelievers are "dead, but not deadly." In other words, the good deeds of unbelievers neither earn the applause of heaven nor the condemnation of hell. They're not good enough to earn the favor of God but neither are they bad enough as to deserve damnation. They're just lying there, corpse-like. Corpses don't earn gold medals but neither do they commit crimes. They just exist. They're just dead. So the scholastic theologians are wobbling on a tightrope. Because the good deeds of unbelievers, are, by definition, good things to do, we cannot condemn them. But because such unbelievers aren't doing them to the glory of God, neither can we approve them. So they want to have their theological cake and eat it, too.

The theologian of the cross, however, says, "No cake for you!" He has a far different, and more blunt, answer. He borrows his response from St. Paul in his letter to the Romans, "Whatever does not proceed from faith is sin," (14:23). In our eyes, an atheist or unbeliever may pull off tremendous acts of love for the neighbor, but in God's eyes, all they do is sin. No exceptions. No loopholes. No special award for trying. No neutrality. Whatever does not proceed from faith—no matter how bright and shiny and loving and compassionate and Nobel-Peace-Prize-deserving it may be—is sin. Thus, as sin, it cannot be "dead, but not deadly," as the Scholastics claim. Rather, because it is sin, it's both dead and deadly. Picture a killing corpse.

As if that were not dire enough, this "killing corpse" doubles down on death by becoming haughty about the whole affair. As Luther writes, "For in such a way, God is robbed of the glory which is owed to Him and it is scattered to others . . . For whoever steals God's glory offends Him, how much greater does he offend who goes on stealing glory from Him and does it proudly," (Proof of Theses 9). In other words, the unbeliever not only sins in everything he does, he boldly glories in being a killing corpse. Instead of giving glory to God, he hordes it all for himself.

If this all strikes you as a being a rather depressing view of humanity, a how-low-can-you-go anthropology, well then, you're right. It is. But it echoes Scripture's rather gloomy epitaphs of humanity. We're barely out of the biblical gate when God points his divine finger downward and says of Adam's offspring: "every intention of the thoughts of his heart was only evil continually," (Gen. 6:5). Notice: every . . . only. Or, as the psalmist says, "The Lord looks down from heaven on the children of man, to see if there are any who understand, who seek after God. They have all turned aside; together they have become corrupt; there is none who does good, not even one," (14:2–3). I like Eugene Peterson's paraphrase of those verses, "God sticks his head out of heaven. He looks around. He's looking for someone not stupid—one man, even, God-expectant, just one God-ready woman. He comes up empty. A string of zeros" (The Message). Even when unbelievers seek to do something good apart from Christ, like offer a sacrifice, it is "an abomination to the Lord" (Prov. 15:8).

Where, then, does this leave us? It leaves us stripped of every confidence that we might have in some good act we've performed. It leaves our lips zipped regarding every boast we might voice about acts of charity, deeds of kindness, or humanitarian prizes we've been awarded. It leaves us naked, dead, humble and hopeless at the foot of the cross. And that's right where God wants us to be. Because there, with Jesus, anchored to him by faith, everything suddenly changes.

All our dead and deadly works are peeled away from us and clenched by the hands of Christ. All our empty, arrogant boasting is lifted from our lips and swallowed by Jesus. He becomes our death, our dead works, our deathly works, all the pseudo-good we imagined we were doing. He not only atones for it, but He transforms it into something else. Because we are in Him, everything we've done in life, prior to conversion and after conversion, is cleansed and sanctified.

If whatever does not proceed from faith is sin, then whatever does proceed from faith is righteousness. If the entire life of unbelievers is sin, then the entire life of believers is righteousness. We have been crucified with Christ. It is no longer we who live, but Christ who lives in us. And the life that we now live in the flesh, we live by faith in the Son of God, who loved us and gave Himself up for us (Gal. 2:20).

What our friends, Thomas, Sandra, and Mohammed, need is not more good works, shinier works, or greater personal sacrifices to make God smile. Not an affirmation that God is pleased with them because of what they do. Not a warning that their works are dead but not deadly. They need what we all need: the word of Law and the word of Gospel. They need to be crucified and resurrected with Christ. And in Him, in this new life in God, the Spirit works in us to do what is well-pleasing to God for the sake of Christ.

Theses 11 & 12

SHAMELESS

BROR ERICKSON

❝ ───────────────────────────────

(11) Shamelessness cannot be avoided or true hope be present unless judgment and condemnation are feared in every work. (12) Before God, sins are truly of less consequence when they are feared as deadly by men.

Theses 11 and 12 of Luther's *Heidelberg Disputation* display the need for both sinners and believers alike to hear the Law preached in all its terror and the Gospel preached in all its glory every Sunday and in every sermon. The Christian never graduates from Psalm 51. We never find ourselves outside the need for repentance. We never find ourselves beyond the need for forgiveness. So the Law must be preached lest we begin to be arrogant before God. The Gospel is preached so that we can continue to live shamelessly before Him.

The danger Luther warns against here is man's assumption he can do good apart from the forgiveness of sins, and thereby trust in his works above the grace of God. This will lead to arrogance and a shamelessness full of self-justification. Scripture is full of warnings against those who would trust in themselves or in the created things as Luther says in his proof of Thesis 11.

Luther himself had experienced this desire to trust in the created things as a substitute for the mercy of God. Unfortunately, the danger has not lifted since his days, even among Protestants who claim His legacy. Rather than Christ lifting the heavy burden and giving us an easy yoke of grace (Matt. 11:30), in the system that Luther reacted against, grace became a burden and a prerequisite for a life of works. A parallel can be seen today when, in modern Christianity, the forgiveness of sins and pronouncement of grace are reserved for and preached to unbelievers, while the Law is reserved for faithful Christians, perhaps under the guise of discipleship.

The reasoning behind such insidious theology is that because Christians already believe, they do not need to hear again that which they trust in: the free forgiveness of sins and imputation of righteousness on account of Christ cruci-fied. Instead, it is believed they should be prodded to do good works of some sort. As regenerate believers, these are possible for them to do now, and because they are possible, they are also necessary if one wants to truly call themselves a Christian. The effect is the same as it was in Luther's own life. Faith in Christ, our sure and certain hope of salvation who alone is necessary and needful, is gradually, and very subtly replaced, and the believer is led to focus on attaining a false confidence in works.

The result of this sort of focus will be one of two: the Christian will either be led to despair, or to shameless arrogance.

If we are lucky, this chain of events will take us down the road of temptation or *Anfechtung* as Luther states in his explanation to the sixth petition of the Lord's Prayer, "lead us not into temptation." Here, Luther says that the devil, perhaps in the form of a preacher, is constantly trying to lead us into false belief which is always a legalism of one sort or another. There are only two religions in this world, Law and Gospel. If a person is not pointed to the death and resurrection of Christ for the forgiveness of sins, he is left to his own recognizance to work out his own salvation. This then leads to despair, and then to other great shame and vice. We are tempted to change the order from the way Luther puts it in his catechism because we assume it is the vice that leads to the despair, but it is despair that leads to vice even if in the end vice will also feed despair. This is why guilt-tripping never puts an end to vice. It only leads to more despair. Forgiveness is the only answer because it takes care of the despair and all of its consequences.

The Gospel can cure despair, but those filled with the leaven of the Pharisees see no need for forgiveness. Therefore theirs is the greater vice, though the world may not see it as any vice whatsoever. One might now ask, are we not back to ranking sins? Just in reverse? No! The sin of pride or arrogance is no less forgivable in the eyes of God, it is only greater in regards to its danger for the sinner. When someone knows they have done wrong they are much more likely to ask forgiveness and even to receive forgiveness before they have asked. But where one is blind to their sin and secure in their false confidence, they do not despair. This is when God must first kill to make alive. "For you save a humble people, but the haughty eyes you bring down" (Ps. 18:27).

Now vice is a word people seem not to grasp today even with the availability of "Miami Vice" reruns or Miranda Lambert's hit song "Vice." Typically the word is used as a category to catch an assortment of unsavory practices one might use to numb pain, assuage guilt, or try to overcome—if ever so briefly—existential angst. Typical vices would include such things as binge drinking, fornication, drug abuse, or gambling. Yet here Luther expands the definition to also include "good" works.

When Luther takes on works, he is not talking about those things that enjoy near-universal recognition as harmful or sinful, such as the vices Miranda Lambert sings about, or Sonny tried to thwart in Miami. These vices typically bring shame along with them. Historically, they are considered mortal or deadly because of the brutality with which they punish their slaves and those around them in this life. And it is for precisely this reason that they are in many ways less dangerous, less deadly, that is, less mortal than the vices to which Luther directs his attention.

There is another way in which man tries to assuage guilt that ironically only leads to sinful pride and more shame, but because the emperor is unaware of his nakedness, he parades around shamelessly. This is the way of supposed good works. They are the emperor's new clothes. We find the righteousness with which Christ clothed us in our baptism and the wedding dress He gave us to be too constricting, too formal. We think we can do better by dressing in our own righteousness. We don't want help from God. We exchange the righteous dress of Christ washed white in the blood of the lamb for that which Isaiah compares to filthy rags. In these clothes that are no clothes at all, we attempt to stand shamelessly before God.

To avoid our fictitious shamelessness, Luther turns to define sins of truly less consequence in Thesis 12.

Of less consequence, this is how people viewed the so-called venial sins in the middle-ages, the peccadillos, small sins that often have little or no earthly consequences. The deadly sins were numbered in succession: pride, greed, lust, envy, gluttony, wrath and sloth. Because of their enormous earthly consequences, they were also thought to have disproportionately great spiritual consequences.

Before God, the sins are most deadly when they are not considered to be so by men. Such a view is nothing more than a miscomprehension of the very nature of sin. It buys into Satan's lie, and succumbs to the serpent's subtle poison that we are free to choose good and evil for ourselves, and ultimately, that we are God. Consider Eve in the garden and how easy it is to miss how deadly such a little sin can be. She partook of a forbidden fruit, but was that really worth subjecting all of humanity to the pain of death and the possibility of Hell? The whole concept becomes a scandal to the hardened atheist. And yet it was precisely in that seemingly little sin of no consequence that the whole world fell under God's curse.

Those sins we shamelessly flaunt in front of the Creator are only a manifestation of the larger problem, and the larger problem is always unbelief. The lack of fear, love, and trust in God above all things. Sin betrays the rebellious soul, even more so when one wishes to trivialize it as something of little consequence that does not need to be forgiven and does not need the blood of Christ.

But the Christian does what God asks and when he is done declares himself an unworthy servant, and receives absolution from the one who came not to be served, but rather to serve. This is why Christ came to save the lost, to heal the sick, to forgive the sinner. We find our salvation in Him alone. In His righteousness, despairing of our own, we stand before God shameless.

Theses 13, 14, & 15

FREEDOM FROM OUR FREE WILL

DONAVON RILEY

"" ———————————————————————

(13) After the fall, free will exists only as a concept, and as long as it acts in accordance with itself, commits a deadly sin. (14) After the fall, free will only has the power to passively do good, but it is always able to actively do evil. (15) Further still, free will could not remain in a state of innocence, much less actively do good, but the will is only able to do good passively.

"Do what is in you." It was a popular late medieval doctrine. If we were to translate the Latin phrase (*facere quod in se est*) into modern English, it would be rendered as, "Just do your best." And what else can God expect from each Christian than that we do our best? Do our best with His grace. Do our best to live a life that follows Jesus' example of holiness. Do our best to live a life of integrity and virtue. The thing is, the more we try to do our best, the worse it goes for us. We jump out of the frying pan of worrying that we have done our best and into the fire of God's wrath.

When we do our best, we imagine that is the purpose and goal of free will. Why else would God give us His commands, for example, if He did not intend for us to do our best to obey them? But here, in Thesis 13, Luther undercuts that whole argument. It turns out, what feels like free will is actually God's wrath. He gives us over to the desires of our heart, as St. Paul says in Rom. 1:24. So, what ends up happening is that instead of "just doing our best" and earning God's grace and favor, we in fact, commit a mortal sin. This is the definition of our bondage to sin.

What our heart wants, our mind justifies. That is our bondage. We cannot accept God as God for us in the way of Christ crucified for the sin of the world. Instead, we imagine that God will reward our best efforts at holy living with more and more grace. The more grace we receive, the holier we become, and on and on it goes until the last judgment. But, for Luther, the fallen will cannot accept God at all. St. Paul says as much in Rom. 7:15–20:

> **For I do not understand my own actions. For I do not do what I want, but I do the very thing I hate. Now if I do what I do not want, I agree with the law, that it is good. So now it is no longer I who do it, but sin that dwells within me. For I know that nothing good dwells in me, that is, in my flesh. For I have the desire to do what is right, but not the ability to carry it out. For I do not do the good I want, but the evil I do not want is what I keep on doing. Now if I do what I do not want, it is no longer I who do it, but sin that dwells within me.**

Our bondage is not that we fall short of doing our best, but instead that whenever we try to do our best we commit a mortal sin. We do not run toward God, but into sin, death, and hell. Free will, after the fall, exists in name only. No matter how much we may want to believe we have a will that is free to choose or reject God, what we call our willing is just sin. We are subject to, and under the authority of sin, and so we are free only to do what is evil. Not that we do not have any will—we do—but it is only free to choose to do what is sinful and evil. We cannot *not* want something. We always want something. But, whatever we want is contrary to God. After the fall, we are in bondage to sin, and therefore not free.

As John 8:34 and 36 says, "Truly, truly, I say to you, everyone who practices sin is a slave to sin. . . . So if the Son sets you free, you will be free indeed." This means that unless Jesus intervenes on our behalf, we are enslaved to sin and it is impossible for us to escape it. Even when we are at our religious best, we still chase after what satisfies the desires of our heart. It follows from this that our will is either bound to sin or to Christ. There is no other way for us to be saved. Everything we do is a deadly sin. Everything Jesus does for us is an eternal, salvific benefit.

So, why did the medieval theologians teach this? Why was Luther vilified and eventually excommunicated for this one assertion in particular? For the same reason that we still push back against Luther's thesis today: doing our best is a defense against God's grace. We refuse to stand in the shadow of the cross. We reject the root cause for Jesus' execution. It turns out that for all our supposed freedom we just cannot accept that we share God's judgment of Israel: "Israel, you are bringing misfortune upon yourself, because your salvation is alone with me." (Hos. 13:9, Translation mine)

It is important to note at this point that in daily life we do have some free will to help and care for our neighbor. But, as far as our relation to God, we have no free will. This is an important distinction for Luther. In our vocations, we are to do our best for the sake of our neighbor. What pants we choose to put on in the morning, what we choose to eat for lunch, and what we do to help our family and friends are all within our ability.

When we come up against God, however, we are confronted by the living God. He is beyond our comprehension. The way we react to this gets at the heart of our problem. We do not like that God chooses us in Christ. We did not choose for God to choose us in this way. Furthermore, we cannot choose this choice for God, on account of sin, but that does not slow us down. We plunge ahead, bound to reject God's free election of us sinners in Christ Jesus. We do not want to live by grace alone, or faith alone, or Christ alone. We want to choose for ourselves how we will live in relation to God. This is why when we "just do our best" we commit a mortal sin because we reject Christ our Savior.

As Luther argues in Thesis 13, our will is not nothing. We do have a will, we do make choices, but in relation to God, those choices are always evil. We are bound to choose to reject Jesus alone, and Jesus only, as our Savior. In Thesis 14, Luther lays out what this means: we must distinguish between what we actively choose to do and what we passively choose to do.

For example, when God's Spirit works in us through the Gospel and His gifts of salvation, good works are produced.

This is what Luther refers to as doing good only in a passive capacity. As we are acted upon by the Spirit, we produce good works. Can we actively produce good works apart from the work of God's Spirit? No. Everything we do apart from the Spirit's work is evil. Therefore, when we are actively trying to do good works according to God's will, we chose everything and anything that flees from and is opposed to, God's will.

Even before the fall, Adam and Eve were created, strengthened, and preserved by the work and Word of God in His declaration of "it is very good" (Gen. 1:31). They passively received the active work of God for them. They were creatures who lived by faith alone in their Creator.

Yet the late medieval theologians always ended up in the same place: the way of our works is the way of salvation. We just need help from God. This was nothing other than the confession of a theology of glory which stood in opposition to the biblical teaching on sin and grace.

The theologian of the cross, on the other hand, "fixes his sight on the passion and cross of Christ." (Thesis 20). This meant that, for Luther, all talk of sin and grace must flow into and out from the cross of Christ Jesus. So, then, for a theologian of the cross, the fall was the man and woman taking for themselves what was not given to them. They tried to claim something for themselves that was not given to them by God; then they attempted to justify themselves (and their works) to God. When we try to understand our relation to God by what we do and leave undone, we are working within a legal scheme that we have constructed to protect us from God. In doing so, we call good evil and evil good. We justify ourselves and condemn God

Further proof of this is that we can actively choose to do something to improve our life, but it will not stop death. Now, "death is the wages of sin." We die, no matter what kind of healthy choices we make. Thus, all our choices (healthy or otherwise) are motivated by sin. But, when we are dead on account of sin, we can only be raised from the dead by someone else. We cannot will ourselves back to life. We can only be a passive participant in our resurrection. We can choose what to change about our life while we live, but we have no power to effect life or death.

Only God can give life, take life, and restore life. After the fall, we believe our purpose and goal is to serve ourselves. We are selfish. We cannot *not* serve sin. Our selfishness is the essence of sin. We do not share God's purpose and goal for our life. There are so many, many people and things we deal with every day. There are fears to be overcome or avoided. There are so many people and things we want to shower with our love. Does God not respect how much time we have chosen to devote to our passion-projects? And, most important, we do this all for God's glory. Our autonomy, it turns out, is what blinds us to the truth of our condition. We will even hold up our autonomy as a sign of God's grace. We confess our sin. We confess our faith. Our sin, our faith. We are responsible for all of it. And this is our sin, the original sin, the sin passed down and recommitted each day, by every person, everywhere, in every generation. This is why only the cross, only Jesus' innocent suffering and death, can free us from our free will.

Theses 16, 17, & 18

ADDING SIN TO SIN

BOB HILLER

" ─────────────────────────────────

(16) The person who thinks that by doing what is in him, he can willingly make himself move toward grace, adds sin to sin in such a way that he becomes twice as guilty. (17) Nor is speaking like this a reason to be hopeless, but causes one to be humbled and seek after the grace of Christ. (18) It is certain that man must give up all hope in his own ability before he is able to receive the grace of Christ.

In his travelogue, *Travels with Charley*, John Steinbeck offers a fascinating account of his attendance at a Vermont church one Sunday. He found a "John Knox" church where the preacher, "a man of iron with tool-steel eyes and a delivery like pneumatic drill, opened with a prayer and reassured us that we were a pretty sorry lot." Steinbeck speaks of the sermon as a "glorious . . . fire-and-brimstone" sermon. "He spoke of Hell as an expert . . . a good hard coal fire, plenty of draft, and a squad of open-hearth devils who put their hearts into their work, and their work was me." This sort of preaching is fodder for spoofing old-time religion in our day. But not for Steinbeck. "I began to feel good all over." He writes, "For some years now God has been a pal to us, practicing togetherness, and that causes the same emptiness a father does playing softball with his son. But this Vermont God cared enough about me to go to a lot of trouble kicking the hell out of me . . . I wasn't a naughty child but a first-rate sinner, and I was going to catch it . . . I felt so revived in spirit that I put five dollars in the plate . . . [this preacher] forged a religion designed to last, not predigested obsolescence."[1]

How about that? Steinbeck is just bludgeoned by the Law's accusations from this preacher, and he loves it! He is not left hopeless or in despair, how could this be? Upon hearing this passage, I found myself wondering the same sort of thing I wondered years ago when encountering Luther's great *Heidelberg Disputation*. Luther's provocative theses come to a remarkable point in Theses 16–18.

Here, Luther hits us with the full force of the Law: you are not a naughty child, in need of correction. You are a first-rate sinner. So sinful are you that if you try to correct your sin and prove to God that you are doing everything in your power to right your wrongs, well, you are only making matters worse. You are adding sin to sin. There's just no way out of it. You are a first-rate sinner.

At least this is the presupposition of God's Word. His Word gets after us and calls us what we are: first-rate sinners. But that's offensive these days. A pastor preaches this too much, he could get sued. See, in our world, we are operating

---

[1]John Steinbeck, *Travels with Charley and Later Novels 1947–1962* (New York: The Library of America, 2007), 818–819.

with an entirely different set of presuppositions that make us look much better and reduce God to our encouraging pal.

Think about how we view ourselves. We presuppose that, deep down inside of us, dwells a really good person. Our job in this life is to find that person, strengthen him with religion, morality, and a healthy diet, until he is strong enough to go before God and say, "I've done the best I can." God, who is certainly glad to help in this process, will see our good efforts, and reward us. Since we suppose that at our core we are good, our pal God won't be able to help but treat us as good people deserve to be treated.

This exposes our presuppositions about God. We think He is the sort of God who wants us to be good, to do our best, and to treat others well. We know, we know, nobody's perfect. But, God knows that too, and He's a pretty nice guy, so He'll throw us a bone. He won't punish us for bad actions so long as our heart is in the right place. If we just do our best, work off those sins as much as we can, we'll save ourselves. He will give us the benefit of the doubt. He'll reward us with a happy eternity in the clouds! We will "obtain grace."

In the midst of this mushy, moralistic dream, that Vermont God shows up with His Law and shatters all of it to pieces. The Law shows up and says, "You are far too gone in your sins to think that you could move towards grace by any power inside of yourself. It's the inside of yourself that's the problem!" We say, "I know I've sinned. But my heart was in the right place!" Perhaps, but once your heart arrived there, that right place was ruined! We are so proud of our religious work and effort; yet that Vermont God preaches, "For out of the heart come evil thoughts, murder, adultery, sexual immorality, theft, false witness, slander" (Matt. 15:19). Or, St. Paul can say in Romans, "None is righteous, no, not one . . . no one does good, not even one" (3:10, 12).

The Word of God is clear: you are a first-rate sinner with no chance of moving towards grace. You ask: But what about all the good I've done? Does it not count for something? Think of my religious devotion, my political stances, my Christian tweets! Surely, God must reward that? The response? Paul can say of his own religious accomplishments and ours, "I consider it all rubbish" (Phil. 4:8).

God's Word of Law gives us no quarter. Even our best efforts to "move towards grace" make matters worse. The trouble is, when we try to effort our way to salvation, we can only do so because we are not listening to the other Word of God: the Gospel. To trust our works in order to obtain salvation is to ascribe to our work that which belongs to Christ alone. His Work is to obtain salvation and to give it out freely. When we put our faith in our works, even our best ones, we turn them into idols and worship them as though they are Jesus.

So, this is why Luther says we must despair of our own abilities if we are going to obtain salvation. Luther, characteristically, gives us two options: Christ or works. If you trust your works, you do not trust Christ and thus prepare yourself for a "squad of open-hearth devils."[2] When it comes to your salvation, God gives His Law so that you will find no hope in your works. His Law works this Godly despair in you (2 Cor. 7:9–11).

---

[2]Steinbeck, 819.

But, notice, then, Luther's remarkable point: Despair is not an end unto itself. We must abandon hope in our efforts, but not give up hope altogether. Why? Because the purpose of the Vermont preacher coming to "kick the hell out of you" is to finally clear your ears to put you into the heaven of Christ's Gospel. As Gerhard Forde says, "In order for there to be a resurrection, the sinner must die."[3] When we try to save ourselves, we add sin to sin. But God condemns our efforts and adds hope to our despair. He gives us Christ!

You need not lose hope because God condemned you in your sin. He only did it so that He would finally get you in the position to listen. And, boy, has He got something to say! You who put your trust in your glorious works, why don't you look away from those for one minute and see what He did for your salvation: He suffered. He died. He was obedient to His Father, not for His own sake, but for yours. You who take your sin so lightly and exalt your works so highly, get over that rubbish. It is nothing compared with knowing this Christ Jesus who had died and obtained salvation for you.

Your best works are your worst idols. But there is no need to despair. For this crucified God loved you enough to "kick the hell out of you," pick your hell up, and carry it to the cross. What's more, He loved you enough to rise and proclaim you forgiven! You are a first-rate sinner. But don't despair. That's just the sort of sinner Christ dies for.

---

[3]Gerhard O. Forde, *On Being a Theologian of the Cross: Reflections on Luther's Heidelberg Disputation, 1518* (Grand Rapids: Eerdmans, 1997), 114.

Theses 19 & 20

GOD AND THE UNWORTHY THEOLOGIAN

DANIEL EMERY PRICE

"

(19) That person is not worthy to be called a theologian who thinks the invisible things of God are observable from events which have actually happened (Rom. 1:20; 1 Cor. 1:21-25). (20) Conversely, a person is worthy of being called a theologian who understands the visible and ordered things of God after fixing his sight on the passion and cross of Christ.

I often think about what it must have been like to be Adam and Eve. To be the only people who know what it is like to be sinless and then suddenly not. To walk with God and then believe the lie that walking with Him and being loved and cared for by Him is not enough. More is desired.

The first sin was and is the desire to be more like God than you are. The Devil's best lie is that you can be like God, that you can know what He alone knows, and that you can see with His eyes. Beware of God-likeness masquerading as Godliness: this is the pursuit that threw all of creation into chaos.

Adam has left an unworthy theologian in all of us: a theologian on a quest to know what God has not given us to know, a theologian of glory. We are all still striving to be God. Still eating the forbidden fruit of wanting to ascend to Him. This unworthy theologian doesn't seek to know God to worship Him, but rather to displace Him. The old Adam in us wants to kill God. We believe God is holding out on us, and that He has kept the best things from us. We associate divine glory with spiritual power. And if glory means power, we will gladly become theologians of the former.

To kill God and take His place we must first understand Him. So, we look to our reason. We obsess over sovereignty, election and why God does what He does and how He does it. Because we are unworthy theologians, we believe we are on some twisted divine Easter egg hunt. We look for knowledge of God in the powerful, beautiful and rational things of the world. But this the opposite of where God has said He is found.

Only a sinner who knows he is a sinner can begin to know God rightly. It's a strange truth that the more one recognizes his sinfulness, the more he understands God. The reason for this is that God has chosen to reveal who He is in the person and work of Christ.

He [Jesus] is the image of the invisible God, the first-born of all creation. For by him all things were created, in heaven and on earth, visible and invisible, whether thrones or dominions or rulers or authorities—all things were created through him and for him. And he is before all things, and in him all things hold together. —Col. 1: 15-17

See to it that no one takes you captive by philosophy and empty deceit, according to human tradition, according to the elemental spirits of the world, and not according to Christ. For in him the whole fullness of deity dwells bodily. —Col. 2:8-9

God, as revealed in Christ, is something the unworthy theologian in us refuses to look at. He doesn't look powerful, beautiful or rational. He looks like the ultimate display of weakness and powerlessness. We agree with the mocking crowd at the foot of the cross: "He saved others; let him save himself, if he is the Christ of God, his Chosen One!" (Luke 23:35) What kind of all-powerful God dies in public? And not a noble death, a shameful one. An ugly, bloody one. It doesn't make sense, and we don't want it to. That isn't what we had in mind when we took the devil at his word that "we could be like God."

But this is who God has always been. He is the Lamb who was slain before the world began (Rev. 13:8). God did not take up this identity after the fall of man. This is who He was, is and will forever be. This is the God Adam and Eve unknowingly asked to be. God will not allow another to take up the sins of His creation. He will instead give the Adam in all of us what he desires. He will let us kill Him. He will die at the hands of unworthy theologians for the sins of unworthy theologians. We look everywhere for God and with our eyes fixed on the heavens miss Him crawling through the streets with a cross on His flesh exposed back. The observable God is locked up in what we refuse to observe. Still, everything we can know about God is wrapped up in the sacrificial Lamb of God who takes away the sins of the world.

Saint Paul states that God has revealed Himself as "foolishness" (1 Cor. 1:18) and "offense" (Gal. 5:11) This same Paul says he preached "the whole counsel of God" (Acts 20:27) and yet says he has "determined to know nothing but Jesus Christ crucified." (1 Cor. 2:2) These are not contradictions. They are the same foolish, offensive truth. To see God and the world He has created rightly is to first observe them through the death of the God who has always been the crucified creator of all things. The God whose glory looks like shame and whose power looks like weakness. The God who reduces Himself to a love that we can hardly bear to look at. But dare to look at the forever slain Lamb of God and keep on looking, that you may become a true theologian, a theologian of foolishness and offense.

A worthy theologian is one who has understood his unworthiness. One who has looked into the darkness of the Old Adam within and seen the desire to kill and be God. One who by grace alone has then had his eyes moved to the crucified God-man, Jesus Christ. One who sees the glory of God wrapped up in His radical love for His murderous creation. One who sees the power of God in the bloody sacrifice of Himself. Real sinners become real theologians by grace through faith in a God who passionately descended to man as a real man. The full counsel of God is only visible in God hanging nude on a tree for a world of unworthy theologians.

Thesis 21

WHEN GOOD IS EVIL AND EVIL IS GOOD

SCOTT KEITH

"

(21) A theologian of glory says that evil is good and good is evil. A theologian of the cross says that a thing is what it actually is.

We are all theologians of glory. We all believe that we have something precious to offer God. Maybe it is our good works; mission trips, teaching Sunday School, helping the poor and downtrodden. Maybe that thing we believe God needs from us is subtler. Perhaps, we imagine, He simply needs our good intentions or our desire to be better. Perhaps, we think, what God needs from us is our faith. And if our faith is not enough, perhaps what He needs is our piety, our complete reverence, religiosity, and desire to follow His will come what may.

We concoct good-work notions and schemes intended to "give God what He needs." These are also meant to convince ourselves and those around us that what we do for God is needed by Him and worthy of reward and praise. We so love praise. We love it so much that we most often lavish it upon ourselves when the world, our family, or the church fails to do so for us.

In pursuit of praise, we even convince ourselves that verses of Scripture, which are intended to show us how much God does not need our help, personify precisely why He needs us. As with Romans 10:4, "For Christ is the end of the law for righteousness to everyone who believes." This means the Law we love so no longer has the power it once did over our lives. While the Law certainly still accuses, its accusation is met with Christ for us saying, "Your accusation has no power. For I have covered this child in my own righteousness."

This then, we say, cannot mean what it clearly says. For surely God needs me to completely fulfill the Law in my life. We tell ourselves and others that He needs me to obey the Sabbath and He appreciates when I do. Surely Paul cannot mean that God no longer needs me to be a good parent, husband, or citizen. Doesn't this passage in Romans merely tell me that Christ has taken away the ceremony of the Law? Certainly, God sees my efforts to fulfill the Law here on the earth and believes they are worth something to Him. And of course, God still needs me to perform the works of the Law. Right?

We as theologians of glory answer every summation and question above with a yes, yes indeed. Furthermore, we see it as our divine duty to perform the works of the Law. And when we do, we wait for God to look upon them and declare them "good." Rather, we call these works "great" and "worthy" and "meritorious" and "righteous" before God has had a moment to gather His thoughts and speak on the matter. We say yes, they are good, they are very good indeed. So, good, in fact, that we can hardly wonder how God ever managed things without them. We convince ourselves of God's reliance on our works so much that relying on them ourselves takes us no more than a half a step.

Yet, this half of a step is a full step in the wrong direction. Maybe more. Reliance, or the assigning of worth or merit to anything we do "for God" is, as Luther said above, calling evil good and good evil. And we are experts at this sort of confusion. It is much harder for sinners like you, and me, to ever admit that God does not need us. He who created heaven and earth by merely speaking, and who sent His most precious Son to save us without our consultations does not actually need our works, our piety, or our religiosity. He needs nothing from us and gives everything to us.

This one-sided reality is what has often been called the Scandal of the Cross. The cross we see as evil and horrid. We cannot imagine that by the suffering and death of the only good man who has ever lived on a horrible tree meant for torture, evil men could be set free. We see this as unjust and deplorable. This is a situation we would never, of our own accord, call "good." Our way says that we get what we deserve. Bad men get punishment, and good men receive their just reward. But we trust in a God who took that earthly logic of ours and turned it on its head in Christ.

In Christ, the evil men receive the reward and the Only-Good-Man, the Christ, received the ultimate punishment. He exchanged His righteousness for our unrighteousness. We contribute nothing to our salvation except for our sin. When we begin to think that we do contribute more than our sin and need for salvation, we are calling evil (ourselves) good and good (Christ) evil. Christ is evil to the theologian of glory because he saves sinners. In truth, good people are none of Christ's concern, He only wants to know and save those who have nothing in them upon which they can rely. This is our Christ.

God in Christ removes our ideas of fulfilling the Law to be saved. He removes our ideas of giving God a pious faith to earn our salvation. In Christ, all our schemes are laid bare and our machinations of self-salvation destroyed.

And so, a theologian of the cross calls a thing what it is. A theologian of the cross confesses, "O Almighty God, merciful Father, I, a poor miserable sinner, confess unto thee all of sins and iniquities with which I have ever offended Thee, and justly deserve thy temporal and eternal punishment." And yet hope through the cross remains for a theologian of glory who admits, often reluctantly, that even the faith which we possess and which we so desperately wish to offer to God as a sacrifice, is not a sacrifice we bring to God, but rather, a gift which He grants to us.

The ultimate lie we theologians of glory tell ourselves is that we are good when we are in fact evil. Then Christ breaks in and breaks our lies. He who claims to be the Way, the Truth and the Life. Even more absurd to us, He claims that no one comes to the Father except through Him (John 14:6). The theologian of glory will boast of his "goodness" though he is evil. Yes, He who is the Truth breaks in with the truth that He is the only way. And that is the truth; He is the Truth. Thanks be to God for destroying our lies and revealing to us truth because of Christ!

Then what do we do with God's declaration of righteousness? The Law calling me evil is not the end of the story for me. It is the end of the story for the "old man" in me. But, God has declared a new me in Christ. That is, I am now *simul iustus et peccator*, at the same time a sinner and a saint who is saved in Christ. "In Christ" I am righteous for the sake of someone else's blood.

So then, a theology of the cross calls us what we are: evil sinners in need of a Savior, and calls Christ what He is: our good Redeemer and only hope for salvation and victory over sin, death, and the power of the Evil One.

God has chosen to look upon you, the glorious sinner, rip your works from your hands, and kill the old man, dead. Then, in a remarkable twist, God declares you righteous for Christ's sake. You have the victory because He said so, not because you contributed. Sorry, theologian of glory, but you are now a sinner made saint!

Theses 22, 23, & 24

THE WISDOM OF THE CROSS

CINDY KOCH

" ————————————————————

(22) That particular wisdom which uses works to interpret the invisible things of God entirely inflates, blinds, and hardens. (23) The Law works the wrath of God, lays slaughter, curses, accuses, judges, and condemns everything that is not in Christ. (24) Yet wisdom is not itself evil, nor should the Law be avoided, but without the theology of the cross, man misuses the greatest things as if they were the worst things.

Why did God put that tree in the Garden of Eden? Many have pondered this question through the ages. This is the tree from which Eve took the fruit, the tree of the knowledge of good and evil. This is the tree upon which the fate of the human race depended. Why would God allow such a tree to exist in His beautiful garden?

God spoke His eternal word, and it was so. This was the beginning of all things. Light was spoken, light was created. Plants and animals did what they were created to do: bearing fruit and living in harmony with their Creator. Man and woman were molded by the hand of God and given the breath of life. Everything that God brought into existence was right and good, very good, in fact.

So it was with that tree with the knowledge of good and evil, right and wrong. There the tree budded, grew and blossomed in God's excellent creation. It sparkled with treasures greater than silver and gold. It swayed calmly in the rhythm of the morning and evening, just as God ordained. It prospered, bursting with the sweet-smelling fruit of understanding. This tree was very good, beautiful and alive, perfectly placed in the Garden of Eden.

Also in the garden lived man and woman. Created for one another, created to trust their God. Believing every Word from His mouth, sustained by every good thing He gave. They enjoyed God's creation, food and protection, comfort and companionship. Yet there in the garden was also that tree with the knowledge of good and evil, right and wrong. A gift of God, indeed, but a gift not given to them.

And the LORD God commanded the man, saying, "You may surely eat of every tree of the garden, but of the tree of the knowledge of good and evil you shall not eat, for in the day that you eat of it you shall surely die." (Gen. 2:16–17)

Why did God put that tree in the garden? If God's Law commanded that man and woman should not eat, why did He put it there in the first place? This very question demands the knowledge and understanding of God. He does not tell us why He placed the tree there, but we are told it is good. He speaks, and it is so. Just as Eve reached up in wonder to taste that glistening fruit, we also can't help but reach out to grasp the unfathomable wisdom and knowledge of God.

Here is where we misuse the best—the good and right and just of God—for the worst. His Law, His commands, His wisdom, His tree: we desire what is God's because we want to be like God, we want to save ourselves. "For God knows that when you eat of it your eyes will be opened, and you will be like God, knowing good and evil." (Gen. 3:5) Attempting to know His secret wisdom, we want to be able to judge what is good and evil. Hoping to discern His right and wrong, we want to take control of our own destiny. What is good when held in the hands of God brings death when we attempt to make it captive to the works of man.

After devouring the first fruit of knowledge, you now feel His commandments press on your heart. You know you shouldn't gossip or lie, murder or steal. You recognize there is a right way to live and a wise path to take. So you look at your works and measure them against the righteous Law of God. You try and seek out life and blessings. You try and discipline your body to conform to His wise decrees of life. You avoid the wicked path to give honor and praise to a holy God. You try to cling to the righteous, glorious path of wisdom that tree had taught us all.

But in your struggle to keep the wisdom of God, the demands of his Law, and the right and wrong of the tree, you only earn yourself His wrath. This wisdom of glory which you seek but cannot have leaves you asking the same dangerous question: Why would God do it this way? Arrogantly, you think you could do the right things God requires. Blindly, you imagine you understood the wisdom of God.

Foolishly, your heart desires to misuse the knowledge of His Law. Although God's right and perfect Law must be done, you are not able to do it. Although you know His penalty for failure is death, there is nothing you can do to escape it. Although you see what the righteous must do to live, your righteous work is not enough.

That good tree, this wisdom, and ultimately, God's Law kill and condemn you just as God said it would in the beginning. It has no power to save you because you cannot do God's Law. No understanding, no knowledge, no work will change your situation. That good tree, this wisdom, and the Law bring everyone death. Every single person since Adam deserves the curse of God's abused knowledge, except for one.

Christ redeemed us from the curse of the law by becoming a curse for us—for it is written, "Cursed is everyone who is hanged on a tree" (Gal. 3:13).

Eventually, the tree boldly displayed what God spoke once we turned our backs on Him: Death. To reverse this word, a sinless Savior was nailed to that tree of man's untrusting knowledge. He who spoke became a perfect sacrifice slaughtered on a tree for our taste of wisdom. On account of Christ, the deadly curse of that tree is destroyed. He was raised from the tomb and gifts us the assurance of eternal life. Now, the tree once bent into a bloody cross is revealed as the tree of life for all who believe.

Although we don't have the answer to why God put that tree in the Garden, we have something better than that. Instead of searching for the knowledge and wisdom that can only bring you death, God shows you the tree that swallowed death. Where every last hope in yourself, in your wisdom, in your works, in your knowledge is rendered useless, a suffering of Christ is your comfort. Where you cower in fear because of the evil your hands are doing, His bloody cross of sacrifice is your focus. Where you are judged and accursed and put to death by the Law, the death and resurrection of your Savior is your life. The wisdom of the cross shames the strong and self-sufficient. The wisdom of the cross brings you to nothing, taking away everything for which you could boast. The wisdom of the cross looks foolish and weak, but it is the power of God for your salvation.

Theses 25 & 26

THE FINAL TURN

ROD ROSENBLADT

" ——————————————————————————

(25) He is not justified who does many works, but he who, without work, believes much in Christ. (26) The Law says, do this, and it is never done. Grace says, believe in this, and all things are already done.

What Luther's earlier theses accomplished was to clear the decks of every sort of false hope we sons of Adam and daughters of Eve use to attempt to justify ourselves before the Holy God. Each is examined and rejected as false. The overall message of them is that absolutely none of them work, that all are false, that each of us has "the sickness unto death," and *there is no cure in sight!*

If this sounds to you like a summary of the first three and a half chapters of Romans, you are correct. Romans 1 is about the utter hopelessness of all Gentile-pagan "answers."

We want to argue with God, "But we had no knowledge, no Book! Go jump on the Jews who *had* the Book!" But God will not accept our excuses and responds: You had the cosmos which spoke enough of Me for you to at least avoid worshipping idols (Rom. 1:18ff.). And you had a conscience within that spoke of at least the basics of the Law (Rom. 2:14–16). Checkmate!

Chapter 2 focuses on the utter hopelessness of all Jewish "answers." Appeals to lineage instead of to obedience to God's law is just another failing "answer." The first half of Chapter 3 exposes that the whole world is under God's juridical righteousness and stands utterly condemned.

Similarly, Luther's first 24 theses of darkness, expose one, non-working "answer" after another, until the reader is utterly checkmated. And reduced to complete silence. You, me, the whole race (minus One) under the verdict "Guilty!" and without excuse.

Years ago, I walked campus with a colleague, a professor of mathematics. He asked, "Rod, what do you think was the greatest discovery during the Reformation?" I responded, "The recovery of the Biblical message of justification by grace alone through faith [in Christ][1] alone, and all *propter Christum*." He responded, "I used to think that, too." What could I do but ask what he now believed? And I did. Dr. Meyer then said, "I think it was the recovery of a true, Biblical view of human sin." That little conversation I have never forgotten—and, I think, rightly so.

Thesis 25 of Luther's *Heidelberg Disputation* is the final turn of it. It had earlier been hinted at, but now comes right out in the open. It is nothing other than the first light of

---

[1] In almost every reference to "faith" I added, in editor's brackets, [in Christ]. This is meant to force the reader to recognize the only object of true Christian faith to be Christ's Person and priestly work *for us*, to be *explicitly Christian*.

hope: justification before the Holy God by faith [in Christ] *sola*—that is, without works! In his proof of it, Luther quotes Romans 3:20 and 1:17, 10:10 later (and I think he could have added Rom. 4:5 as well!).

This does not just sound incredible; it is shocking to us all. It sounds like crazy-talk. It sounds like St. Paul writing about "a righteousness not based on Law?!" Think of how an audience of lawyers would respond to such a proposal. Any true answer would have to be constructed out of "earning, wages, virtue, works, etc." Such things would be the only legitimate coinage, no?

Luther contrasts what Scripture says with Aristotle and his discussion of "becoming righteous." One becomes a builder by building, becomes an instrumentalist by practicing instruments, becomes temperate by performing temperate acts, brave by performing brave acts, etc. *And righteous by doing righteous deeds!* (See details in Theses 29–40) Who can deny that this is consummate human wisdom?

But Luther charges into this fray, using Scripture. Righteousness before God comes *only* by hearing about Christ and believing into Christ. To attempt to "become just" by performing acts of justness/justice is to overlook the fact that we are not capable of works solely for the sake of neighbor. We are much too inwardly polluted to do such pure things! Instead, we need to pursue "the foolishness of God which is wiser than the wisdom of the world" (1 Cor. 1:25). As Luther states, "He who is without works but believes much in Christ is righteous before God!" (Rom. 4:5).

Too, Luther was concerned that there be no confusion between the righteousness of faith and the works that will indeed follow. Luther argues that these are not the believer's own. They are God's (using us as God's vessels or instruments). Any time we are looking for some sort of "confirmation by looking inward" we will find nothing but sin and death again! The Reformers wrote that sin could be described as "*incurvatus in se*" or turned in oneself. The only way of confirmation is to turn our gaze *outwards* to Christ's Person and work (and in particular His dying *for us*). The Father raising Him after three days was not only for our justification. It was the Father's way of saying that He accepted the work of the Son *for us.*

Thesis 26 defends that the Law is right, is "holy, true and good" but also that the Law *cannot* bring about in us what it demands of us. It "works wrath and keeps all men under the curse!" It can curse, but it *cannot* bless (in the sense of enabling us to do what it demands). The Law can only point helplessly to that which it cannot produce. All of this, Luther scholar Gerhard Forde calls "standard Pauline and Augustinian teaching."[2]

Is there anything in this teaching that is more positive? Yes. It is the theme, "Grace says, 'believe in this,' and everything is already done." Or, paraphrasing, "Faith [in Christ] *nude, sola, without works,* justifies sinners before God!" Luther quotes Augustine: "And what the law commands, faith [in Christ] obtains."

---

[2]Gerhard Forde, *On Being a Theologian of the Cross: Reflections on Luther's Heidelberg Disputation, 1518* (Grand Rapids, Mich.: Eerdmans, 1997).

To any theologian of glory, this language seems utterly hyperbolic at best, and, at worst, quite dangerous. After all, what will happen to human moral earnestness if people get wind of the claim that through faith [in Christ] all has already been fulfilled *for them?* But this makes sense to any theologian of the cross. And Luther held that if there is any faltering here, all is lost! He pushes the language to the limit, refuses to "back off." He insists that faith [in Christ] does not have to be prompted to do good works because in faith [in Christ] everything is already done. Preposterous as it sounds, it is based not on us but rather on Christ who has fulfilled all things *for us.* As Forde puts it, "The point is precisely that the power to do good comes only out of this wild claim that everything has *already* been done."[3]

Why should any Christian take the time to read Luther's *Heidelberg Disputation?* Because it will profit him or her in questions that we all have regarding the relationship between our imagined "good works" and point us in another direction: that is, again to Christ's Person and work *for us.* It will clarify for any reader the nature of justification (always a helpful aspect!) and could, for many, comfort the troubled conscience (a key theme throughout the Lutheran *Book of Concord*).

---

[3]Forde, *On Being a Theologian of the Cross.*

Theses 27 & 28

LOVE FOR THE UNLOVABLE

WADE JOHNSTON

" ——————————————————————

(27) Actually one should call the work of Christ an actively functioning work and our work is a completed work,[1] and thus a completed work which is pleasing to God by the grace of Christ's active work. (28) The love of God does not find, but creates, that which is lovable. The love of man is made up of those things which it loves.

The tax collector entered the temple a sinner in the eyes of all but went home justified (Luke 18:14). Zacchaeus the outcast was called to climb down from a tree and host the most Holy God in his ill-gotten home (Luke 19:5). Demons were cast out of Mary Magdalene who later became one of the first to proclaim the resurrection (Luke 8:2). Saul was knocked off his high horse as a persecutor of the church as part of his commissioning to take its message throughout the known world (Acts 9:1–19). Peter was told, "Get behind me Satan," so he could witness Jesus' path to the cross and then herald all that it means for the lost and broken (Matt. 16:23). The

---

[1] *Operatum*

Gerasene demoniac, his tormentors cast into swine, became the only sane man in town (Mark 5:15). Mary, chosen from obscurity, sang of the God who exalts the humble and humbles those who exalt themselves—as Jesus put it later, that the first will be last and the last first (Luke 1:46–55; Matt. 20:16).

Luther wrote, "The love of God does not find, but creates, that which is lovable. The love of man is made up of those things which it loves." These are perhaps some of the most beautiful words ever written. They cut to the heart of the Scriptures. They turn theology, philosophy, and human experience on their head. They run counter to natural love—that love that comes naturally to us after the fall. Humans are capable of amazing love, but even our best falls well short of what Luther describes here. We are bound to reciprocal, *quid pro quo*, self-interested love of varying degrees. We love because we have a connection with, get something from, like something about, or have an appreciation for something about another person or a cause into which they somehow fit.

This is not to downplay the great feats of love recorded in our personal histories and throughout human history which humans are still capable of after the fall. It is, however, to be honest, to call a thing a thing, and to state matter-of-factly the case in a fallen world. People are capable of various kinds of love (familial affection, friendship, and romantic love, for instance), but people love people because they find something lovable in them, have some real or perceived obligation toward them, or some personal benefit from doing so, even if that personal benefit is the ability to feel good about helping someone else. Luther here describes something else entirely: "The love of God does not find, but creates, that which is lovable. The love of man is made up of those things which it loves."

Luther laid the groundwork with the thesis before this. He explained, "Actually one should call the work of Christ an actively functioning work and our work is a completed work, and thus a completed work which is pleasing to God by the grace of Christ's active work." Luther and the Lutheran Confessions distinguish between two kinds of righteousness, civic and divine. The first is active, what people do (all people), the second is passive, what we receive from God through faith as Christians. Similarly, we can speak about good works in two ways. We can speak of good citizenship and we can speak of the obedience of faith. Regarding good citizenship, a person is good in his neighbor's eyes because he does good things. Regarding the obedience of faith, a person does good works because he has been declared good, righteous, in God's sight, this for the sake of Christ who was crucified for sinners. The first sort of works spring from all sorts of natural, human motivations; the second sort are baptismal. They are a product of our daily dying and rising, the work of Christ for us, in us, and through us, by His Spirit, given to us in the sacrament. Read Romans 6 and consider Luther's explanation of Baptism in the Small Catechism. These are works, not of that old, begrudging obedience of fear, the religiosity of the old Adam, but of newness of life, of our adoption as God's children.

Soon after Luther's death, a debate broke out about whether good works are necessary for salvation. Things got heated, quickly. Thankfully, the biblical teaching held the day. The consensus formed that good works are necessary, but not necessary *for salvation*. Good works are necessary because God commands them. Good works are necessary because good trees bear good fruit. Good works are necessary because faith, the gift of God, is a living and active thing. But these good works aren't done under compulsion. They're done freely. They aren't done so that God will love us. They're done because He loves us. They aren't performed in order for us to be saved (in fact, they aren't a performance at all!). Rather, they flow from our salvation, orchestrated, not for show, but by God and for our neighbor. They are the product, not the cause, of our salvation, an accomplished fact, as certain as the crucifix.

Here, in our works, Christ, who claimed us in Baptism, now wears us as His masks, uses us as His hands and feet, makes us channels of His love for those around us. We often don't even realize it. In fact, these works often seem unimportant and unimpressive, even as Christ's seemed so to many in His day. As we ponder Christ's love for us, though, freely given, totally undeserved, we are moved by Christ to love our neighbor. He accomplishes His works through us. And so we love our neighbor with works done with confidence in God's promise, not for fear of punishment or out of anxiety that God who so freely gave will quickly take away what Christ died to make our own.

Even as we are surely saints through faith, because we are still sinners this side of heaven, our works, even the best, are still stained and imperfect. As with our person, so with our works: God receives them as perfect in His sight through Jesus, our Jesus (He who saves, continually so). In short, these are works that flow from a realization of our dependence upon Christ and not from some hope of needing Him less. They are the result of being drawn deeper into His grace, not some sort of progress toward needing it less—that would be a move away from, not toward our God. Our works are motivated by God, not meant to motivate God. Otherwise, they would be what Jesus condemned in the self-righteous, not what the Vine has promised to produce through His branches. The works of faith are a demonstration of Christ's love for us and for our neighbor worked through us, not a measuring stick by which we gauge His love for us. We need no other gauge than the cross.

"The love of God does not find, but creates, that which is lovable. The love of man is made up of those things which it loves." When I teach freshmen theology, I ask my students, right out of the gates, why God loves them. I put the same question on the first few tests. There's a specific answer I want to drill into them. It's a pretty simple one: "Because He does." We like to think there's something in us, something we have or do or think or inherit that sets us apart, that contributes in some way to God's love for us. God's love, however, is perfect love, undeserved love, true charity, and we dare not want it any other way. Otherwise, it becomes fickle, uncertain, a bargain and not a promise—human love, the kind God became man to transcend, not to imitate. God loves us because He does, and thank God for that! We are lovable because God loves us, and what better reason could there be?

Jesus came, not to call the righteous, but sinners (Luke 5:32). And that's precisely what He's done, again and again and again—the tax collector in the temple, Zacchaeus in the tree, Mary Magdalene, the demoniac, Saul, Peter, you, and me. The righteousness that avails before God, that counts in His sight, that saves, is gift and all gift, from faith to faith, of faith from first to last (Rom. 1:17). This realization changed the course of Luther's life. This beautiful truth forms the bookends of his powerful Heidelberg theses, and, in Christ, our lives. You are loved by God, because He loves you. You are loved by God and He will use you as He sees fit, once again, because He loves you, and because He loves your neighbor. This is life in a world given back to us, not as a treadmill, but as a penultimate and impermanent home returned to us, not to idolize, but to enjoy, a place to love, serve, explore, create and appreciate creation, all with the righteousness of Christ, confident of His love, through the freedom of the Gospel.

MEET THE AUTHORS

STEVEN PAULSON

Steven D. Paulson is professor of systematic theology at Luther House of Study, Sioux Falls, South Dakota. He is an ordained pastor of the Evangelical Lutheran Church in America. Paulson is a Summa Cum Laude and Phi Beta Kappa graduate of St. Olaf College, Northfield, Minn., and earned the master of divinity degree from Luther Seminary in 1984. He holds both the master of theology (1988) and doctor of theology (1992) degrees from Lutheran School of Theology in Chicago.

CALEB KEITH

Caleb Keith holds a B.A. in theology and classical languages from Concordia University Irvine and is currently pursuing an MA in systematic and philosophical theology from the University of Nottingham. Husband to Erika Keith and father to their two children Esther and Emerson. He is the producer of the Thinking Fellows podcast and the director of the 1517 podcast network.

DAN VAN VOORHIS

After receiving his Ph.D. in modern history from the University of St. Andrews, Dr. van Voorhis spent 11 years teaching history and political thought at Concordia University Irvine. He speaks nationally in academic and general conference settings and is a published author on subjects ranging from the Reformation to the Enlightenment and Cold War. He is producer and co-host of the Virtue in the Wasteland podcast and the author of *Monsters*.

KELSI KLEMBARA

Kelsi is a freelance writer and the editor of the 1517 Blog. She is currently pursuing an M.A. in Reformation studies from Concordia University Irvine. She lives with her husband, Doug, in Dallas, Texas.

LARRY HUGHES

Larry Hughes is a member of Our Savior Lutheran Church in Danville, Kentucky, where he serves as head elder. He is a contributor to the book *Wittenberg Confessions—Testimonies of Converts to Confessional Lutheranism*.

CHAD BIRD

Chad is an author and speaker devoted to honest Christianity that addresses the raw realities of life. The Gospel is for broken, messed up people like himself. Whether he's writing or speaking, his focus remains on God's Good News for our world: that Jesus is the friend of sinners. He was willing to give his life that we might have freedom and forgiveness in him. He holds master's degrees from Concordia Theological

Seminary and Hebrew Union College. He is the author of *Night Driving: Notes from a Prodigal Soul* and *Your God Is Too Glorious*. He is also a regular contributor to Christ Hold Fast and 1517. Chad and his wife, Stacy, enjoy life together in the Texas Hill Country.

BROR ERICKSON

Rev. Bror Erickson serves as pastor of Zion Lutheran Church in Farmington, New Mexico. He graduated from Concordia University Irvine in 2000 where he studied apologetics under Dr. Rosenbladt, and Concordia Theological Seminary in Ft. Wayne, Indiana in 2004. He likes to translate the works of Bo Giertz and Hermann Sasse. He also enjoys writing reviews on Amazon and critiquing modern culture with the Gospel.

DONAVON RILEY

Donavon Riley is a Lutheran pastor, conference speaker, and author. He is a contributing writer for 1517, Christ Hold Fast, and LOGIA. He is also the co-host of The Banned Books podcast and the As Lutheran As It Gets podcast.

BOB HILLER

Rev. Bob Hiller is the senior pastor of *Community Lutheran Church* in Escondido, California. He is a regular contributor to The Jagged Word and 1517 where he writes on sports, theology, or whatever might be bothering him at the time.

DANIEL EMERY PRICE

Daniel is the Director of Christ Hold Fast. He is an author, church and conference speaker, co-host of the podcasts

40 Minutes in the Old Testament and *30 Minutes in the New Testament*, and he leads the interactive online *Bible Study For Normies*. Daniel has served as a church planter, pastor and worship leader and currently lives in Bentonville, Arkansas, with his wife Jessica and daughter Anna.

SCOTT KEITH

Dr. Scott Keith is the Executive Director of 1517 The Legacy Project and Adjunct Professor of Theology at Concordia University, Irvine. He is a co-host of *The Thinking Fellows Podcast* and a Contributor to The Jagged Word, 1517, and Christ Hold Fast blogs. Dr. Keith is the author of *Being Dad: Father as a Picture of God's Grace*. He earned his doctorate from Foundation House Oxford, under the sponsorship of the Graduate Theological Foundation, studying under Dr. James A. Nestingen. Dr. Keith's research focused on the doctrine of good works in the writings of Philip Melanchthon.

CINDY KOCH

Cindy is wife to Pastor Paul Koch and mother of five busy children in Ventura, California. In between homeschool and church events, she writes for 1517 and The Jagged Word. She is a conference speaker and has an M.A. from Concordia Seminary St. Louis in exegetical theology.

ROD ROSENBLADT

Dr. Rod Rosenbladt (Ph.D., University of Strasbourg) was a professor of theology at Concordia University in Irvine, California for over 30 years, and has contributed to numerous books and recorded presentations. He is also an ordained minister in the Lutheran Church-Missouri Synod (LCMS).

WADE JOHNSTON

Dr. Wade Johnston has degrees from Martin Luther College, Wisconsin Lutheran Seminary, Central Michigan University, and Erasmus University Rotterdam. He serves as assistant professor of theology at *Wisconsin Lutheran College* in Milwaukee, Wisconsin and served for ten years in parish ministry in Saginaw, Michigan.

www.ingramcontent.com/pod-product-compliance
Lightning Source LLC
Chambersburg PA
CBHW021933040426
42448CB00008B/1048